LOVE YOUR DISEASE

Where there's smoke...

John Harrison, M.D.

Where there's smoke

Prologue

This book focuses upon the habit, or the addiction, of smoking. However, the principles upon which the book is based apply to all habits, and to all addictions.

In going through these pages, please substitute any of your own personal habits or addictions that are causing you a problem, for smoking.

If we don't address the role of our own personality, it's virtually impossible to fully resolve any addiction. Those addictions may include smoking, prescription opioids, over-eating, alcohol, sex or any other habit that's a problem for us.

The most difficult addiction to resolve is the addiction to being "right", a consequence of the need for control. This shows up as rigid views and opinions, and often masks a deep-seated criticism of ourselves and others.

We may need to re-consider our current attitudes and opinions, and become available for exploring elements of ourselves and life which we previously regarded as "facts".

This book signposts just such an exploration.

John Harrison 2017

Where there's Smoke is the third book in the *Love Your Disease* series. The first book in the series, *Love Your Disease It's keeping you healthy*, explores the role of our own personalities in the cause and cure of disease, and the second, *Highway to Health*, explores using our current circumstances to provide the insights that lead to recovery.

Introduction

How many times have you been congratulated for smoking?

How many times have you been criticised by yourself, other people, doctors, your family or the anti-smoking lobby for smoking?

Right now in our lives, every time we smoke we confirm to ourselves or to others that we're non-deserving, we're weak or that we suffer from some personality defect. Think of the accumulated health effects of all that criticism.

What if the difficulty in quitting smoking was a consequence of the criticism, and not the nicotine?

What would it be like if, every time you lit a cigarette, cigar or a pipe, you reaffirmed to yourself that you're an honourable person doing the very best you can in this most difficult set of circumstances called life.

Accepting ourselves for being addicted to life-threatening habits like smoking or opioids, requires a willingness to question what you believe right now.

What a phenomenal change to your well-being accepting yourself might make.

What if you not only stopped criticising yourself for smoking, but you used your smoking to actually improve your health.

This book helps you do just that.

Table of Contents

		Page
Prologue		3

Chapter

1	Choices	8
2	There's something wrong with me	15
3	The Child adapts	28
4	Safety First	37
5	Realities	41
6	Emotions	45
7	Smoking away those Feelings	62
8	Habits and Addictions	69
9	Breathing and Smoking	81
10	Smoking with Love	87
11	Becoming aware of Criticisms	94
12	Being a Smoker	99
13	Thinking about Smoking	103
14	Accepting Smoking	112
15	Loving the Smoker	116
16	Smoking as a Problem	127
17	Loving Smoking	130

Epilogue	133

Chapter 1

Choices

We do all sorts of things….marry, go bushwalking, change jobs, take holidays, wash our hair, fight with our neighbour, change TV channels, paint the house, take drugs, yell at the dog and smoke cigarettes……*for very good reasons.*

Often we haven't a clue what those reasons are, but that doesn't invalidate them.

Much of the time we do things without thinking, and some of these we come to regret. However, if we consider the pressures upon us at the time, some of which we may have been aware of and others that came to light later, we begin to realise that we did the best we could. In an evolutionary sense, it may not even be possible to do less than our best.

Sure, with 20/20 hindsight we would've done it differently, but at the time all we had was our 10/20 real time sight!

So how come we're criticising ourselves for this episode from the past?

Perhaps we're still experiencing the fallout. This could be left over feelings such as anger, sadness and fear, or the many variants and combinations of these basic emotions, such as remorse, regret, guilt, discomfort, anxiety or panic. We don't like feeling these emotions and since we attribute them to the event we regret, we say that the decisions we made then were wrong.

Like taking up smoking back whenever.

And yet, perhaps our unwillingness to feel those emotions is the real problem, not the earlier decision. We claim that if we'd made a different decision we'd be avoiding the uncomfortable feelings and be feeling happy instead.

"If only I'd resisted that affair," we claim in desperation at our deteriorating marriage, finding our current feelings of sadness and despair intolerable.

"If only I'd held on for a few more years and hadn't sold the business at the bottom end of the market", we try and convince others, "I'd be a millionaire by now".

"If only I'd taken more care of my diet when I was young I wouldn't be suffering from arthritis now", we exclaim, trying to contend with the feelings of anger or frustration from being immobile.

"If I could only take back that one comment to the boss I'd be senior vice president as we speak", we claim in remorse.

"If only I'd married her when I had the chance", we lament.

"If only I hadn't turned my ankle at the critical moment it'd be me up there on the victory podium."

"If only I'd known about the drinking before I married him", a woman claims, "I'd be so much happier than I am now."

"I wish I'd never taken those narcotics prescribed by that doctor", we exclaim, forgetting our suffering at the time.

"If I'd never met that group of friends I'd never have started smoking"

However, despite our later claims to the contrary, all those decisions were taken using the data and the information we possessed at the time, whether we were aware of it or not. More importantly perhaps, we made them given how *we were* at the time.

Hindsight, additional information gained over the intervening period isn't much good when you don't have it. Furthermore, we wouldn't even be in possession of the hindsight had we not made the original decision. We only know more now *because* we made the earlier decision. The old decision, the object of our complaint, also provides information which helps us do something different now.

Smoking was the best thing to do at the time, and the same goes for whatever we're doing now, whether we're smoking or not.

Why do we do things which we declare at a later date to be a "wrong" decision?

We're a different person now. We've grown and matured. We only grow and mature by deciding things, doing things and experiencing the consequences, and some of those very things which were invaluable to us in learning and growing are the very same things we're regretting now.

We needed to do them.

We've used them to shape our understanding of us and our world. We've used them to test our own independence, to step hesitatingly from the protection of childhood to the responsibility of being a grown up. They have been, and continue to be, an integral part of our lives and our personalities, for everything we ever did contributes to us and our potential happiness and health, much as we may want to deny it.

Everything.

Now if this is true, and we may be unwilling to accept that right now, why would we keep claiming otherwise? Why would we keep criticising a particular event and perhaps our involvement in it. Why would we keep admonishing ourselves for continuing to smoke, for example? If smoking has been, and continues to be a beneficial activity, why would we keep criticising smoking and ourselves for partaking in it? Perhaps we don't see any benefits from smoking, especially in the light of so much criticism of smoking and smokers, and the obvious health risks.

Perhaps we need something to be critical about?

Could it be that we need something about which to criticise ourselves?

Somehow we Humans have learned to criticise ourselves, criticise others and a lot else besides. Why do we need to be so critical?

If the purpose of our smoking is to have something to criticise ourselves about and we stop criticising ourselves, what will happen to the smoking?

We may not immediately identify with criticising ourselves, and are more comfortable criticising others instead, or attributing the things we don't like to factors beyond our control, the "life sucks" attitude. In this last case we're critical of life.

Some of us don't recognise self-criticism, having buried it beneath our tendency to criticise others.

In order to remain in denial of this we may be attracted to moralizing about other people's lives. This makes denial so much easier. Judges, lawyers, doctors, politicians, Government departments peopled by individuals claiming to act in the "public interest" are often living out this denial of self criticism and replacing it with the judgement of others.

Anti-smoking organisations may attract such individuals who attack smoking without ever questioning what greater hazards may replace it.

Society chooses certain activities to be critical about at any point in time.

Right now smoking is one of the bête noirs of society, roundly condemned by everyone, those who smoke and those who don't. Obesity is another.

And it's not just the medical profession who've decided that smoking causes.... (too many diseases to list here!), for there are other reasons for smoking currently receiving such a bad press and treatment by the courts.

These reasons are to do with personal responsibility.

A battle of blame is being fought over smoking.

Governments wanting to reduce spending on health, propagate the belief that smoking is the responsibility of tobacco companies. This justifies windfall taxes from tobacco.

People smoke for many reasons with varying degrees of compulsion. From pure pleasure on the one hand to relieving the anxiety and stress of contemporary living on the other; from making social interactions easy on the one hand to escaping the problems of poverty on the other, to name a few.

In order to be universally condemned, the benefits and advantages of smoking need to be overlooked, ignored or denied, and the perceived disadvantages need to be highlighted.

For the health of all smokers it's important that they not be caught up in the frenzy to blame someone, either themselves or anyone else.

But this book goes further than alleviating the guilt and self-criticism of smoking. We intend using the very act of smoking to assist us to improve our health and well-being.

Chapter 2

"There's Something Wrong with Me"

Smoking may be taking the brunt of our self-criticism now, but there may be underlying criticisms which smoking helps us avoid.

Let's take a look at some common criticisms we make of ourselves and where they came from. We all criticise ourselves and we all criticise others. This is normal human behaviour. Some religions believe that criticism guarantees being born in the first place, for Earth is the place where you come to work through your criticisms. If you manage to shed your criticisms in this lifetime, you don't need to be reborn. Others believe that we're born critical of ourselves and this serves to keep us humble.

Do you recognise any of the following?

"There's something wrong with me"

"I should be better"

"I'm not good enough"

"I ought to have this sorted out by now"

"I keep making the same old mistakes"

"I'm too weak to give up smoking"

"You'd think I'd know better by now"

"I should've done it differently"

"I'm bad because….."

"I'm hopeless when it comes to quitting"

"What's the matter with me!"

All these statements are an attack upon our self.

These criticisms are so fundamental that they may perhaps be regarded as a Human signature without which we don't qualify for residency on planet Earth. Animals may not have the same self-criticisms. Our whole life may be no more (or less) than finding ourselves in circumstances that bring us face to face with our own criticisms. Those people who use these opportunities to resolve their criticisms achieve peace in this lifetime. The rest of us suffer the consequences of these leftover criticisms which range from disenchantment with life to physical and psychological illness.

A fascinating component of criticism is that we attack ourselves to the same degree that we attack others, though we may be adept at disguising either. This makes a lie of self-aggrandising individuals who claim to know what's best for others. Beneath that self-promoting exterior lies a frightened child, always running from the fear of not being good enough.

We can use any aspect of our lives to flag our unworthiness.

Here are a few:

Health

"What's the matter with me?"

"What's wrong with me?"

We believe that we ask these questions as a consequence of suffering from an illness, but the reverse may be true. Because we believe that there's something wrong with us we become ill. The illness then confirms that indeed there's something wrong with us.

> **Criticising ourselves for smoking may contribute as much to disease as smoke particles, nicotine or tar.**

Any belief, attitude or opinion rigidly held restricts the normal functioning of our immune and endocrine systems, making illness more likely and recovery more difficult.

Our own body's healing mechanisms attack or nurture us to the degree we attack or nurture ourselves. Autoimmune disease, in which the body attacks itself, may be the consequence of longstanding and deep seated attacks by the individual upon himself.

But back to some common areas of self-criticism.

Money

We may claim to have too little, too much, or have poorly managed our resources.

If we're driven to acquire wealth in order to keep away from the underlying belief that, in this case, we're not good enough if we're poor, money may not liberate us much. The criticism will eventually be re-assigned from money to some other area of our lives.

Body Image

"I'm too fat, thin, bald, short, tall, ugly, slow............."

"My bottom's too big, stomach's too fat, my ears stick out, my breasts are too large, my penis is too small, hair's too thin, nose sticks out, my chin's too weak, my shoulders are too small, my knees too knobbly, my skin's lousy, my eyes are too close together, my skin's wrinkled ….."

Have I missed you out?

Feel free to add your own. They're all judgements, and here's the rub, none of them are "true". Oh, of course you think they are, live your life as though nothing else could be truer, but these criticisms only serve to fulfil an underlying self-criticism that needs to find expression in something. We need to pick something…anything… to fulfil our underlying Human pre-requisite that: *"there's something wrong with me"*.

We achieve membership of our tribe by these criticisms, which is one reason we're reluctant to part with them, however damaging they may be. Anyone doubting this might spend some time in a ward in a hospital, where membership of the group is retained by being sufficiently sick to remain in hospital. *"I'm sicker than you are"* prevents you being expelled from the group.

Self Image

"I'm exceptional, I'm a real plodder, I'm confused, slow, dumb, a poor public speaker, a brilliant lover, a smart-arse, uncultured, uneducated, hopeless at math......"

"I'm not good enough"

"I'm better than others"

"They're not good enough".

It doesn't matter much whether the criticism is "positive" or "negative" or whether it applies to us or to someone else, ultimately it comes back to judgement itself. Criticism and judgement, per se, is the lot of us Humans.

Sexuality

"I'm no oil painting, I have premature ejaculation, I never orgasm, I'm a pervert, I like looking at other people doing it, I have almost uncontrollable urges, I'm the world's most boring lover, I'm guilty of looking at other women, homosexuals are disgusting, nudity is wrong, I never feel satisfied, my genitals are ugly…."

In a society dominated by sexual guilt and implications of wrongdoing, sexuality is a common receptacle of our feelings of unworthiness. If anyone or any organisation in a position of power wants to be rid of a competitor, alleging sexual misconduct is a sure-fire way of doing it. Even though everyone may know that the allegations are self-serving, we all run for cover lest we too, are branded with sexual impropriety.

Currently, men are being invited to feel an abhorrence of their gender. Boys as young as six years old are being punished for "sexual harassment". Ads on television portray men as useless, insipid creatures who can barely manage to function in the light of their uncontrollable and infantile sexual urges. Women are portrayed as expedients and dilettantes, tossing out partners the moment a wealthier or more powerful prospect shows up. Everywhere we look misanthropists persecute the public as a way of denying their own personal guilt, deeply hidden as it is, particularly from their own view.

Children

If the resolution of self criticism is the psychological imperative of life, then arguably having children is the biological imperative.

Most of us feel as though we could have done better rearing our children. We all tried to correct the mistakes our own parents made with us as we saw them, usually discovering at a later point that we made the same "mistakes" as they did. If we did manage to do something different with our own kids, the practice we desperately tried to avoid usually skips a generation and then re-appears. A woman reminded me of this when she said that as a consequence of being raised in a large family where her needs were ignored, she limited her own family to two children, and devoted herself to them. As they grew she noticed that they were indifferent to others' needs, brought up as they were to expect everything would be done for them. "Have I really done my children a favour?" she rhetorically asked me.

Relationships

Nothing comes close to relationships as the perfect opportunity to run our stuff.

Few of us would claim that our relationship with our partner or partners has no downside, and if a sustained period of marital bliss occurs, we usually engineer some cock up to drag us back to the main game, i.e. the resolution of the belief that "there's something wrong with me", "there's something wrong with you", "there's something wrong with us" and "there's something wrong with life."

Let's take the situation where we aren't in a relationship and want one. What do we say?

"I just haven't found the right man yet, I'm not ready to settle down, I can't seem to attract the girls I want, women find me too boring, all men know that women feign attraction to gentlemen but go home with rough trade, men just use you and then throw you out, women are always looking for the main chance, I think I'm destined to be alone".

Again, come up with a few of your own.

We have two families in our lives.

The first is the family in which we grew up. The second is the family (or families) which we create as grown ups.

The latter family has a tendency to reflect anything unresolved in the former, so that all our left over frustrations, resentments, hostilities, aggravations, insecurities and self criticisms we acquired as a child come back to visit us as grown ups. We often attribute these old attitudes and beliefs to our current relationship but they're mostly leftovers from our first family. If we don't recognise this we're in danger of viewing what's happening in our immediate family as independent of our existing beliefs and that usually leads to conflict. Hence a man who accuses his wife of being unfaithful may be acting out what happened in his own first family where that was either the belief of his own father or perhaps the practice of his mother. The boy believes "women are unfaithful"….. and his wife's a woman. He has something negative to say about either his wife, who he believes is having an affair, or about himself whom he believes incapable of holding onto her. He believes that he's observing present time "fact", whereas he's really only regurgitating a belief he acquired as a child, a belief well past its "use by date". It was acquired at a time which no longer exists.

He may trade the first wife in for a new one who also reflects his unresolved first family issues, therefore gaining nothing. Statistics from failed second marriages suggest just this.

Because of the closeness and the intimacy of relationships, they have great potential to bring up old stuff that was acquired under similarly intimate circumstances, i.e. a child and his parents, particularly his mother. They are by nature, emotive. Adult relationships are the next time in life where we hope to be looked after perfectly, as we'd hoped for in childhood, with the likelihood that we'll be equally disappointed this time around.

The opportunity of relationship is to recognise where our beliefs come from and stop attributing them to current circumstances. Of course our beliefs may accurately *reflect* the current situation because we're attracted to this current situation because of its potential to put us back in touch with the earlier difficulties. It also provides options to resolve them. To take this a step further, the man who believes his wife is unfaithful may be trying to make her unfaithful by setting up circumstances in which she has the opportunity to stray. He needs his beliefs about women confirmed. Usually he won't have to try too hard, since one of the reasons he was attracted to her in the first place was that he detected in her the capacity for infidelity.

Why would he do this?

Because it makes him feel safe.

How come?

He prefers the pain and suffering of his wife's infidelity to the fear of having to re-appraise one of his core beliefs which is that "women are unfaithful".

And what's so frightening about dropping that belief?

If the belief was a significant theme in his childhood, the child may have needed to adopt that belief in order to get cared for, at least as he experienced it at the time. Jettisoning the belief risks disapproval. As a child he wouldn't have known that adopting a particular belief was critical to attracting caring, but it was one of a number that he acquired by rote. No child is in a position to disagree with a core parental belief or a belief which arises from a parental action. It threatens to lose him caring and that's life threatening. As a grown up, letting go of a core belief results in the old anxiety and uncertainty which surrounded the original adaptation. *Women / men are unfaithful* is a core belief.

We seem to be attracted to partners who are as critical of themselves and of us as we are of ourselves and them. A huge disparity in the area of criticism would prove intolerable for both parties.

When it comes to smoking, reflect a moment on what you say about yourself smoking, and about your partner smoking. What does your partner say about her smoking and about you smoking? This can be a pretty interesting exercise. It often reflects what partners think about each other and themselves, smoking aside.

Thank goodness for the smoking, otherwise we might have to confront some pretty raw areas of our relationship.

Our habits are a common way of attacking ourselves and others.

Habits

"Man, how long have you been saying that you'll get up early and go for a run!" we say in self-disgust.

"Look at these nails. You'd think I'd have stopped biting them by now. I am 60 years old!"

"I tried. I really did. If the boys hadn't come over I wouldn't have touched a drop"

What do you say about your own smoking?

Here are a few I've heard over the years.

"I wish I could give the bloody things up"

"I had my chance six months ago. I'd stopped for nearly a year, the longest time ever"

"I'm just too weak and that's the truth"

"It's a filthy habit!"

"My constitution's really strong, so I can get away with it"

"What! The price has gone up again! You'd have to be an idiot to keep smoking, so what does that say about me!"

"It's too late to stop now. The damage's done"

"I'm just too anxious to give up"

"If I give up I'll blow up like a balloon like I did last time. At least I'm not grossly overweight, that ought to count for something."

How do you personally use smoking to criticise yourself?

Take a while to consider this and write down some thoughts for later reference.

Now, as an exercise, apply the spirit of these criticisms to yourself without invoking the act of smoking to justify the criticism.

As an example:

"It's too late to stop now. The damage is done" might be applied to any other activity, let's take work. Our statement made about smoking as applied to work might look something like: "There's no point changing jobs at my age. I'm too old to get another job". If looked at with no object of the criticism, neither smoking nor work, but directed at ourselves, our criticism becomes something like: "I'm hopeless. I just can't change".

Simply removing the reference to smoking is revealing. "It's too late to stop smoking" becomes "It's too late." We may feel as if life has passed us by and that it's too late to have anything be different. Smoking may be masking resignation or even depression.

If we're not ready to confront more fundamental criticisms of ourselves, we can smoke until we are.

Now where do these criticisms actually come from? Let's take a look.

Chapter 3

The Child Adapts

In any twenty four hour period a four year old child receives, on average, over 400 "negative" messages and less than 40 "positive" messages. From this experience the child has little option but to believe that "there must be something wrong with me", since she can't seem to please mum and dad. Remember, we've discussed how criticism seems to be a fundamental characteristic of the human species.

These negative messages are everyday comments delivered routinely by parents.

"How many times do I have to tell you to pick up your clothes!"

"Can't you see that mummy's tired?"

"Hurry up or you'll be late for school. We've been through this routine every morning this week!"

"Stop making a noise sweetheart. Daddy's been at work all day and he's got a very bad headache"

The child can't seem to please her caretakers, therefore she concludes that she's not good enough. If she were perfect, exactly as she is, she'd be totally approved of.

Also, if the little girl were perfect she'd be able to make mum and dad perfectly happy, and much as she may try, she can't seem to do that. More confirmation that she's not good enough.

Please note that this is normal parent – child interaction in Western civilization. I'm not saying that it should be any different.

Remember how as kids we were aware of some dissatisfaction or unfulfilment in one or both our parents. Maybe you can remember trying to do something about it.

The child is shaped by his parents who are passing on what they were taught by their parents, older siblings, peers and society.

The child puts aside his own needs in order to attain caretaker approval. He needs the approval of his parents since they keep him alive, and in his early years he has no option but to take notice of them. He may not do what they want, but he must take notice of what they want, as his safety depends upon it. Then he assesses his risk, and complies or rebels.

Children are prepared to trade their lesser needs for those which are life sustaining. The life sustaining needs are food, warmth, shelter and perhaps to a lesser degree, cuddling. Since we can't provide any of these things for ourselves in our early years, securing these needs is life sustaining. We trade other needs for the essentials, and this forms the basis of adaptation.

We become who we are, rather than who we might be.
We limit our potential in order to please.

We learn to adapt in order to attract approval and love. Parental love comes with certain viewpoints attached, and we have no option but to settle for the conditional love of our parents since that's the only love available. It doesn't matter much whether we comply wholeheartedly with our parents' view or whether we reject it. We're still responding to it, adapting to it.

Our need to adapt causes us to believe that there must be something wrong with us, for if we were perfect, we wouldn't be required to adapt at all.

Children have no platform or experience from which to judge parental behaviour. If it comes with the threat of withdrawal of parental love if the child doesn't comply, children make the decision to adapt and survive.

To appreciate the child's position, try this exercise.

Select something which you love doing.

Now select something which you dislike doing.

Imagine that conditions are perfect for indulging in your favourite pastime and you can't wait to get started. Someone comes along and forces you to drop what you want to do and do what *they* want you to do, one of your most disliked activities. The catch is, this person keeps you alive, so if you know what's best for you, you'll swallow your *desires,* and follow your *needs*.

How are you feeling whilst you're doing this?

Resentful, annoyed, furious, resigned?

All these feelings represent anger. And with whom are you angry? The person forcing you to do what you don't want to do, of course. But whoops.....that person keeps you alive, so whilst you may be grumbling away at him inside, expressing anger at him or her seems unsafe. What do you do with the anger instead? With whom do you get angry?

There's only one person with whom we can safely be angry.

Us.

We turn the anger towards parents into ourselves, criticizing ourselves for being so imperfect as to not attract perfect parental love. Anger directed at oneself is the basis of guilt.

Take a couple of simple examples:

A father may have approved of his son only when the boy was the best player on his basketball team. Now a professional basketball player, the young man criticises himself every time he misses a shot, believing that he deserves it, because he should do better, and that keeping on his own case is the way to being a better player. He reckons that this is "logical", not recognising that he's simply regurgitating, unwittingly, his father's admonishments.

A young girl was only acknowledged when she helped her mother care for her younger siblings. Now grown up, she feels guilty every time she puts her own needs ahead of someone else's, complying with her mother's old intimation that she should selflessly devote herself to others. She finds herself attracted to nursing as a career, or to a sick husband, neither of which fulfil her.

Anger directed inwardly shows up as guilt, and the words which accompany it are "I'm not good enough" or "I should do better". Or something like that.

We won't remember much of the circumstances that lead us to adapt to parental pressure and to become self-critical, as often the parental directive is implied or modelled, rather than delivered directly. A father for example may never tell his son not to cry, but he never cries himself, modelling to the boy that "men don't cry". Nor does it matter whether the criticism is positive or negative, the child adapts to it.

We've said before that this is normal Human childrearing leading to normal Human behaviour.

We grow up with things we say we don't like about ourselves, about others and about life, and we spend much of our life attracted to circumstances which are capable of fulfilling two essential requirements.

- The circumstance confirms what we already believe.

- The circumstance brings the old conditioning to the surface and provides us with the opportunity of freeing ourselves from it.

In other words, the very existence of a problem gives us an opportunity of resolving its source.

Were we to be living totally in the present, we wouldn't have any problems, at least nothing we'd define as a problem. Until we have no problems, the current problem is:

We're living in the present but run by the past.

What do *you* criticise yourself about?

Think about this awhile. Remember, a "positive" judgement or criticism is as significant as a "negative" criticism.

Anyone come up with smoking?

If not, feel free to list your own.

As kids we turned the anger we felt when we didn't get exactly what we wanted towards ourselves, encouraged or invited to do so. This took the form of guilt and self criticism and initiated an ongoing climate of self-judgement and perhaps self-attack.

Once we've concluded that there must be something wrong with us because we receive conditional and not unconditional love, we establish a belief system and ultimately a world which confirms that belief. A lifetime of defensive attitudes, beliefs, opinions and self-images takes form. They're defensive because we adopted them for protection in the first place, and they remain our attempt at controlling our environment as grown ups.

I repeat. This is normal human upbringing.

These defences and adaptations are incorporated into our personalities and into our physical bodies, which is why some people appear physically open and others are obviously defended against the world, perhaps doubled up or hunched as though they're always ducking to avoid the next missile life sends their way. The defences become our "reality". Where someone else may see an effort of ours as deserving praise, we see it as needing improvement. When a comment is passed as to how well we're looking we take it to mean we looked awful before. We distrust the approval of others.

Conversely, we may judge what we do to be superior. This is the same fear of not being loved if we don't fulfil a parental requirement, in this instance to be better than everyone else.

We set up everything in our life to confirm our beliefs and our reality. We construct our self-image, (or "brand" as it's now known in the highly visible Internet environment) relationships, business, health, success, finances and habits to demonstrate the "truth" of what we already "know". We associate with others with whom we share "agreed upon fictions", declaring them to be facts, or truths.

Any habit we can't easily break, such as smoking, serves to prove that we're weak, we're anxious, we need support, we're under attack and we need defences. This is not all we use smoking for, but in this chapter we're looking at some of the benefits of smoking given the childhood adaptations which we all, smokers and others, had to make.

In the current climate of antagonism towards smoking by practically everybody in the community, smoking serves to invite attack from others.

Everyone's use of smoking will be different, but here's a few different lines of inquiry which you might find worthwhile pursuing.

What would happen if you stopped being so hard on yourself?

Are you a person always looking for a challenge?

Do you find a certain emptiness, or aloneness, disquieting, leading to a smoke?

Do you like to go through life in a fog?

Are you smoking to avoid unwanted thoughts of inadequacy or unwanted feelings of anger, disappointment or sadness?

If you're a person who attacks smokers and smoking, are you using the attack on others to avoid your own feelings of inadequacy? Does this make you feel superior?

Are you smoking to help you "keep your nose to the grindstone", frightened that if you slacken off you'll fail to achieve the wealth and status which you crave?

We'll be coming back to these and many more questions which our smoking poses as we proceed.

Chapter 4

Safety First

Imagine that you're a tiny baby, having just arrived from the security of the womb. You find yourself in a massively different world where you know none of the rules.

You're now dependant for survival upon other people who have their own needs to attend to, and these needs often take precedence over yours.

We struggle to adapt to this new Universe, trying to make it smaller and more manageable so that it seems safer. We grab at any method of getting our needs met, putting aside the less important in order to guarantee those which keep us alive. We try and learn the rules that will get us best cared for as quickly as possible, since we can fulfil none of our needs ourselves.

Since we have no experience, we're in no position to judge the merits of our parents attitudes, so we just do whatever gets our needs met, including adopting a whole bunch of their beliefs and opinions which, were we adults, we may completely disagree with. The attitudes we adopt in order to attract caring as a child become our "reality".

Our need for safety as children accounts for the determination with which we still cling to our old belief systems as adults, for they *were* life sustaining when we adopted them, and may *appear* life threatening to abandon as adults. The adaptations which we accrued as children form our personality, and we're reluctant to give them up now since at least they have a proven track record.......they've kept us alive thus far, whereas any alternative, attractive though it may at first appear, has yet to demonstrate itself capable of sustaining us.

Children can't trade in their parents, and their need to adapt is self-evident. But why, as grown-ups, don't we just get rid of any left over adaptations that no longer serve us?

Whilst the child needs parents and family to survive, grown ups need partners, friends, acquaintances and probably most importantly, the community, for well being. We acquire our friends and acquaintances because of our opinions, attitudes and beliefs, carried on from childhood mostly. If our reality differs too radically from our tribe, the relationship falters and may end altogether.

Whilst we don't need these people to keep us alive, the grown up might find life not worth living without his world being peopled by others of similar beliefs. That's why we're reluctant to move too far from the known. In days gone by, loss of the tribe meant that we died.

Smoking has provided us with many things. Smoking allays anxiety, provides social contact, fills up the void in our lives and enables us to belong to a social group. And we're still alive. How do we know that we'll survive giving up!

Intellectually, of course we know that we can survive giving up smoking, but this is not an intellectual exercise. We smoke for reasons of safety (as well as pleasure), and our safety is never trivial.

Just as we created a reality as kids and we're reluctant to give up that reality as adults, so smoking has become part of our reality, part of our defences and adaptations to a world which is not that easy to handle. If we could give up the belief systems we adopted as kids with no repercussions, the world would be peopled by enlightened beings, living entirely in the present. But it isn't. The world is populated by people struggling to throw off the shackles of yesterday in an attempt to better survive today.

The world is a place where we criticise our honourable attempts to survive.

If the child had no adaptations to make, if he were cared for perfectly, he'd never question his worthiness to survive. Perfect caring is of course impossible. Perfect caring means that as soon as the child had any need at all, that need would be instantly and fully satisfied. Breast milk of perfect temperature and consistency would be delivered before the baby suffered the pain of hunger. Warmth, cuddling, cleaning, and all comforts would be delivered as soon as the need arose. Since this doesn't happen, the child is forced to consider how to best fulfil his needs. Adaptation is the answer.

The *reality* which we adopt as kids, including our attitudes, beliefs, opinions and all those things of which we say we're certain, restrict our capacity to function in the present. They also restrict our capacity to respond to a threat.

Our immune and endocrine systems are responsible for relating to our fellow travellers in life (viruses, bacteria, the weather, pollutants) and for correcting anomalies in our internal chemistry. The way we think and feel about ourselves affects our internal physiology. This medical science is known as psycho-neuro-immunology, the science of the connection between our psyche, our nervous system and our immune system.

The degree to which we find ourselves restricted as adults by old leftover childhood beliefs, is the degree to which our immune system is restricted in its attempts to heal us in the present. By keeping our viewpoint narrow, out of a need for safety, we keep our healing narrow. Physical disease is made more likely, and recovery more difficult.

Chapter 5

Realities

Our defences and adaptations, consisting of attitudes, beliefs and opinions become fixed in childhood, and we're reluctant to give them up as grown ups. These attributes become our personality or our second natures. "Oh. It's become second nature", we say in reference to a trait of ours repeated so often it's become part of us. All of these attributes, consisting of thoughts, emotions and actions, constitute our reality.

We don't realise most of the time that what we regard as "real" is no more than a thought associated with a feeling. We don't realise that we're actually thinking. We deal with our own thoughts as though they're universally true, meaning that they apply to everybody, everywhere. Our thoughts become our reality. Hence a man who was taught as a child that men don't hug each other believes that he "knows" this as an adult. He treats this individual belief that he accepted in his own upbringing as a universal truth, as "fact". When he travels to Asia, Spain and various other countries, and sees Policemen and men in the Armed Forces walking down the street holding hands, he's a bit shattered. At first he's repulsed. He may then realise that what he regarded as a universal fact is nothing more than something which he was taught and which he now regurgitates, for safety. (He may never stop thinking that it's *wrong*, however)

Why this persistent belief?

Because he adopted the idea that men don't touch each other in order to be approved of as a child. Parental approval kept him alive. His father didn't touch his own boys. In order to be approved of by his father, he took up his view. Had our man been born elsewhere, he may regard holding hands with another man as normal. Fear of disapproval drives children to adapt. As adults, this same fear maintains the belief system, because we mostly congregate for safety with like minded individuals, our community or our tribe. To despatch a belief is to risk being disapproved of firstly by ourselves, and secondly by the like minded individuals in our tribe. Both disapprovals are dangerous to us. This stops the man mentioned above from holding hands with his peers who were brought up with the same prohibition to touching another man as he was himself.

If you're a man who belongs to a community group such as a sporting team and you sat next to a team mate and held his hand, imagine the outcome.

Similarly, you've probably already experienced the fallout from being a member of a group of smokers, and deciding to quit.

Our defences, personality or ego is our defence against the world, adopted in childhood.
Defence implies the presence of attack. If there was no attack as a child we wouldn't have developed the defences and if there was no attack as a grown up, we

would have lost them over the years. If we still have them, attack exists. Attack means a threat to us.

Where does this attack we fear come from?

We've said that we attack ourselves with thoughts like "I'm not good enough", "I should be better", "What's the matter with me!" If we believe and experience life as a place in which attack can be expected, we need to create a world in which our expectations are met. We need to live in a world which thinks of us as we think of ourselves, i.e. deserving of attack. If this were not the case our internal reality "I'm not good enough", would be at odds with our external reality "The Universe approves of, supports, and loves me". Such a reality schism would be intolerable. An example might be a person who believed he was male whilst everyone else treated him as a female. Withdrawal and psychosis would result. So we match our external circumstances with our internal reality, as in the following example.

A country which spends $2 billion a year on defence has a $2 billion belief in attack. A country which believes that attack is not possible won't spend a cent on defence. Furthermore, a country spending $2 billion a year on defence is likely, sooner or later, to initiate a war in order to justify its expenditure. There are plenty of examples of this.
If someone suggests disbanding the armed forces because there have been no recent wars, pandemonium breaks out as people's fears come racing to the surface. Once a defence is in place and has become "reality", we don't like dismantling it. It's too frightening.

Defences cannot be changed by intention. They resist too strongly.

Defences acquired as children change when we no longer try and change them and focus instead on accepting them and accepting ourselves for having to acquire them in the first place.

When we reduce our attack upon ourselves, we invite less attack from outside in order to keep our internal and external reality in balance. Our defences can then similarly reduce.

Berating ourselves about smoking does not help us stop smoking.

When we come to accept that every single thing we've ever done in our life was done for the most honourable of reasons, namely to look after ourselves as best we could given the circumstances, then any activity we're undertaking for the purpose of criticising ourselves will disappear, of its own accord. So too will any activity we're engaging in for the subconscious purpose of harming ourselves. Conversely, if the activity is of no harm to us, then it will not disappear.

If you can recall a concern of yours that disappeared of its own accord, you may be able to recall that you became engaged in some other pursuit or project which made the previous concern redundant. You didn't try and get rid of it. It went when you no longer needed it, apparently of its own accord.

Chapter 6

Emotions

We've been considering the impact of critical *thoughts* on smoking. Now we take a look at the relationship between *emotions* and smoking.

The passage of a ship through rough water is made smoother by its stabilisers. Similarly, a motor vehicle travels more easily over rough terrain because of its shock absorbers. Nether of these devices are intended to eliminate feedback of the ocean or the road entirely, since this is valuable information. They merely cushion the impact and make the journey more comfortable, as well as offering a degree of safety for the passengers.

We have similar devices for smoothing our passage through life, relating to our environment, balancing our physiology and communicating with other people we meet along the way. These are our emotions or feelings.

The four basic emotions are anger, sadness, fear and joy. There are many others, some of which are combinations of feelings that make up a complex range of human responses to our environment. Anguish, disgust, anxiety, irritation, pique, martyrdom, misery and many more consist of either combinations of anger, sadness, fear and joy, or partially expressed emotions which have not been permitted to complete themselves and, as a consequence, remain trapped inside the mind and body.

Emotions have psychological and physiological consequences.

For health, an organism needs to be employing all its survival and health regulating devices, and for humans, emotions play a large part in balancing body physiology. Most of us suppress one or more of our basic emotions to some degree, which means that we're denying ourselves access to our full healing capabilities to the same degree. Many of us are much more comfortable *thinking* than we are *feeling*. Our tendency to over-ride an *emotion* with a *thought* can be gauged by asking yourself the following question.

"What do you feel about poverty in the developing world?"

Was your answer something like:

"The developed nations need to get way more generous towards the third world."

Or, was your answer along the lines of,

"Sad and angry".

Did you answer with an emotion, as you were asked, or did you answer with what you ***thought,*** and not what you ***felt***?

Many of us will have answered with what we *think* about poverty in the developing world, as we've become accustomed to discounting emotions and valuing thoughts. The modern world of business, technology and finance rewards people who can perform with minimal emotional and maximal logical, unemotive thinking.

Many of us are so repressed in our emotional states that we're unaware of feeling anything. We may notice the external signs of emotion in others, but be unaware of them within ourselves.

Anger and fear are both part of the "fight or flight" response and have major physiological consequences, such as increased heart rate and cardiac output, sweating, dilatation of the pupils and a redistribution of blood flow to organs taking part in the fight or flight. Joy announces itself by facial expression, at least in children, though masked in adults much of the time, and sadness, which naturally would involve crying, tends to be suppressed, particularly in men.

The nervous and immunological systems are activated when we express an emotion and are dulled when we don't. For health they need, like any other system in the body, to be exercised, and then allowed to rest. We get problems from not exercising them at all (suppression) and from over exercising them (emotional indulgence or "racket" feelings). This latter might be the case with someone who appears to be always angry, even over minor matters, such as occurs in much "road rage".

What's the relationship between smoking, and expressing or repressing emotions?

Most of us light another cigarette whenever our nicotine level drops below a level at which we feel comfortable. Nicotine is only part of the story but let's start there. The act of lighting up has become automatic, and only comes into consciousness when we have no cigarettes left, or when we're deliberately trying to cut down or stop smoking. Then we get to feel the edginess or anxiety of not having a cigarette, but most of the time we never let ourselves get to that point because we light up before we reach it.

What emotions lurk in the underworld concealed by our smoking?

If you're willing, stop smoking for however long it takes you to get in touch with those feelings. For some people this might be about fifteen minutes, and for others a day or so.
Now you need to ask yourself what you're feeling. Remember the four basic emotions of anger, sadness, fear and joy. Is it any of these, or is it one of the many combination feeling states? Can you identify it? There may be quite a few emotions.

Most of us have a range of mechanisms to deal with not smoking which similarly suppress whatever we're feeling. Eating, exercising, watching TV, working, chewing gum, having sex and many other activities also serve to avoid feelings, so during this exercise, try to be available for any feelings to show up.

Were you able to detect any?

Yes?

No?

The result of expressing an emotion fully is a healthy mind and a healthy body. If we get in touch with a feeling but don't allow it to run to completion, we end up changing an acute (immediate) emotion into a drawn out (chronic) emotion.

Drawn out anger tends to accumulate and leads to violence. Sadness which is partially expressed and becomes chronic turns into misery. Instead of a good cry we end up being half sad half of the time. Acute fear turns into chronic anxiety and if joy is not allowed to be expressed fully we tend to bottle it up and end up half smiling and half crying.

Smoking is one of many methods humans use to suppress emotions.

The most common method of suppressing emotions is to *think* instead of *feel*.

If we totally suppress our emotions such that we're not aware of them at all, we may develop a physical disease, depression, or both. It's very important to our well being that we find out if we're avoiding emotions. The willingness to express ourselves varies within cultures. Some of us are unwilling to express much, the typical "sang froid" of the English, whereas the Latin races are much more willing to express themselves. I found this out in the middle of a Rome winter many years ago.

I was driving my Fiat home at 2am and it was snowing. I stopped behind a car at a traffic light on a slight incline. The car in front rolled back into my car. I realised that there was minimal damage, I didn't speak Italian, and it was freezing outside, so I stayed put. After a few moments the driver in front got out of his car and came towards me waving and gesticulating, and when I sat there in stunned silence he began banging on the roof of my car. I realised that I hadn't done the acceptable thing, so I got out, yelled a bit, pointed animatedly at my car, and within a few moments he was satisfied, got back into his car and drove off. He had initiated an expression of emotion when he didn't get one from me, and no doubt within hours or days he would have completely forgotten about the incident because for him, it was complete. As for me, I'm recounting it 30 years later!

How do you start practising the basic emotions after a lifetime spent suppressing them?

Slowly, is the answer to that question.... slowly.

Let's take a look at them.

Anger

Anger has a poor reputation because of a failure to distinguish between *natural anger* and *violence*, which is anger focused towards somebody or something that we claim "made us angry". In the latter case the person who's feeling angry takes no responsibility for his emotion and wants to blame somebody else for it. The anger is not resolved by doing this and builds up until it finds expression in violence.

The following is an example of anger in nature.

Imagine an animal which is attacked by another animal. Notice the fierce snarl and growl it displays towards the aggressor. It has the appearance of anger, but it doesn't give the impression that the animal is *furious* with the aggressor, or blames if for being angry. Such a concept is nonsensical. The animal which is growling is afraid of either losing something (food, territory or a mate usually), or of being invaded, and it adopts as fierce an expression as possible to let the other animal know that it will be no pushover should a fight eventuate. It's demonstrating the fight component of "fight or flight". Once the incident is over, the animal holds no grudge towards the other animal and has no intention of seeking retribution. It has responded naturally, and the aggressor expects no less of it.

Anger release

If we yell loudly, lie on our back and beat our fists into a mattress, and kick our feet vigorously, or take up a tennis racquet or soft baton and beat a mattress, soon the anger takes over and whatever we were angry about, disappears. In a therapy setting this is referred to as an "anger workout". The anger has gone, at least temporarily. With most people, multiple sessions of anger release are required.

If, whilst doing an anger release, the person with whom we're angry stays in our mind, then we haven't completed with the anger and may have to return to it at a later time. In the first instance the anger is over and done with, and in the second, it isn't. Anger which is not completed but which builds over time, is obvious to others, if not to the person who's angry. Such individuals have the appearance of a fuse about to blow. They may become increasingly ruddy and their blood pressure keeps rising. Eventually they invest all the left over anger in someone or something, often themselves, and cause damage. This is called violence and resolves nothing. The consequences are often serious for all parties. Because of the failure to differentiate between anger which retains an object and is not release, i.e. violence, and natural healthy "fight or flight" anger, *all* anger has been criticised by many authorities as dangerous.

Is smoking keeping your anger at bay?

Smoking takes care of difficult emotions. Quitting before you're ready may leave you worse off, for now you need another outlet for those emotions which underlie the smoking.

A better proposition may be to use the smoking, or whatever else it is that you're doing to avoid anger, to allow yourself to slowly get in touch with it. Each time you light up a cigarette allow the act of lighting up to alert you to the fact that you're probably using smoking to suppress an emotion. Use any other habit or addiction to alert you to emotions you're trying to avoid.

Stopping smoking prematurely is akin to throwing the baby out with the bathwater.

If we're going to let anger play its natural part in our emotional makeup, we'd better find out something about it. Let's take a look at some aspects of anger.

Nobody "makes me angry".

Anger is a naturally occurring healthy emotion which needs expression and completion, like thirst. You can no more say that someone "makes me angry" than you can say that someone "makes me thirsty". The anger is ours, not theirs. Whatever they've done or said is the trigger for our anger. If we were carrying around no anger within us, we wouldn't become angry with them whatever they said. In this sense people can't "make us angry" because we're angry already. People can't make you thirsty and they can't satisfy your thirst. The same goes for anger.

The first step in resolving anger is to own it.

The next is to not make someone wrong for what they, with their own needs, have done, even though their needs may conflict with ours. Their act may have triggered our anger, but there's no point claiming that we feel like we do because of them. We were already feeling like that, deep down, though possibly outside of our awareness.

"I'm never angry at what I say I am."

Boy, this is a huge leap of awareness for most of us, for we like to claim that we're angry because..........

Much of the time, our defences or ego never allows us to be in touch with what really angers us because that would reveal that we're angry from years ago, right back to childhood usually, and to allow ourselves to be in touch with that is too raw and too frightening for most of us. So we cover the original anger with some latter day justification for being angry.

Our anger is often of the "Hey you, ...whaddaya looking at!" variety.

In other words we invite someone else to relate to us in a way in which we feel justified in being angry back. We tailgate the driver in front of us on the freeway till he jumps out at the next traffic light and threatens us. We leap out and protest: "Hey, wha'd I do?" and then get into a fight justified by his unreasonable behaviour. We deny the fact that we were feeling furious already, perhaps because our partner had belittled us once again, at our insistence, (to continue with this theme), if we want to be honest about it.

Sadness

Most of us don't have to think too hard to decide if we allow ourselves to cry or not. Women usually do, and men usually don't, at least in some societies. When we do cry it may be over some minor thing that we care little about, as the tears are really coming from deep inside us from a long time ago, when the little boy or girl who was us was sad and lonely.

A good cry feels really great. It's not difficult to arrange. Go get a tear jerker video or two and sit at home alone if you're too embarrassed to cry in front of others, and, armed with a box of tissues, bawl your eyes out. Ah…wonderful.

The consequences of not crying are often recurrent upper respiratory diseases such as sinusitis and rhinitis (constantly runny nose). Tears have antibacterial properties (apparently), so a good cry gives the upper respiratory tract a good washout.

We said earlier that partially suppressing sadness leads to its chronic counterpart, called misery.

What's the relationship between smoking and misery do you think?

Smoking may be used to suppress sadness.

Maybe cigarette smoke isn't the only cause of red eyes and swollen mucous membranes. Maybe smoking stops us from feeling the emotion of sadness, and not feeling sadness also causes red, itchy and irritable eyes.

Have a good cry and find out.

Fear

It's difficult to imagine anger without fear preceding it. If we weren't afraid in the first place there would appear to be no sense in getting angry.

Both anger and fear are part of the "fight of flight" response, and cause major changes in our body physiology.

We get fearful if we're threatened with loss or invasion. Animals are the same. The loss for animals is loss of territory, food, mate, shelter...the real basic survival needs...meaning that the animal fears for its life. For humans the basic needs are already catered for much of the time so we get frightened at other losses, the most basic one is the loss of love, or approval. As a child the loss of love would have meant death, since the child is unable to keep himself alive in the first years of life. If he survives, it means that however bad his parenting was, there was at least sufficient love to keep him alive. As a grown up, a threatened loss of love brings us into contact with the same fear we had as a child. Of course as a grown up we can now keep ourselves alive without any assistance from others, but without love, either from a partner, family or from the tribe, would we want to stay alive?

The other threat is the threat of invasion. Humans and animals are fearful if they're physically threatened. This must have been one of the first and most fundamental parts of the brain to evolve for without it, we would not have survived for very long.

Our first response in fight or flight is fear, immediately followed by anger as we try and give the impression that the consequences of messing with us could be serious. I've been unable to think of a situation in which anger is present without underlying fear. If you can think of one, please contact me and let me know. Fear however, seems to be able to exist without anger.

We often try and avoid fear. Anxiety, apprehension, panic, concern, wariness, hyper-vigilance, alarm and trepidation are names given to fear, some of which represent a dilution of fear or a mixture of fear and another emotion. Excitement, for example, is a mixture of fear and joy.

Smoking is one of the most efficient ways of alleviating fear, which is why it's been used by humans for a very long time.

Nearly all serious addictions, be it prescription opioids or illegal narcotics, are an attempt to avoid fear.

This book helps us to use smoking as a way of slowly addressing our fears, rather than compounding our self criticism and subsequently both our anger and our fear. Smoking has been assisting us on some fundamental level for otherwise we wouldn't have taken it up and we wouldn't have continued with it. Criticism compounds our belief in attack. When we experience attack we feel fear followed by anger. What might we be fearful of? Let's begin by addressing our contemporary fears.

Are there any matters in your life now that are frightening for you? You need to spend time and be honest with yourself about this, as much of the time we deny fear, and so your first response may well be, "Hell No!" Take your time getting beneath this knee jerk response.

What's frightening about this matter?

What are the potential consequences?

What's the worst thing that can happen to you if your worst fears are materialised?

Does this consequence remind you of anything which happened to you as a child?

What was it?

What was the consequence of it?

In considering the fears in our lives now, we'll be drawn back to childhood fears which we've yet to resolve.

A boy who was required to be successful in order to attract parental approval recalls an incident when he was 9 years old and brought home a report card showing he'd achieved 98% in math.

"What about the other 2%?" was his father's only comment.

Striving for perfection, the boy grows up to be the senior vice president of a large multinational organisation.

He admits to no-one, much of the time not even to himself, that his success has not come easily, for he regards himself as an under-achiever, despite the evidence, and is constantly striving to attain a degree of approval which of course, will never be forthcoming. Without being aware of it, he's trying to get perfect parental love. Underlying his attempt is the fear that if he's not perfect and unable to attract perfect love, he may not survive, an out of date belief which still runs him. For similar reasons, very wealthy people may accumulate more and more wealth, though it makes no difference to their level of comfort. When their wealth makes no difference to the harsh judgement they pass upon themselves, they delude themselves that their problem is a consequence of not being wealthy enough.

Exercises in Fear

There are many psychotherapies and bodywork therapies that assist people in rediscovering and re-experiencing their fears. Many of them work on the premise that the re-experiencing of the fear decommissions it. Others say that the old emotions are not accessible and only present time emotions are worth freeing. Like most things there's probably truth in both approaches, and like most things, some people do better with one approach than with another.

Most of us can get in touch with fear by a few simple exercises.

The first is a lot of fun and involves going to an amusement park and taking on the scary rides. Open your mouth and scream. Ever noticed how girls dominate the most frightening rides at amusement parks? Why? Because they're less controlled than boys. Boys don't scream as much and as a consequence they end up greener, or worse! Enjoy.

The second exercise involves making out that you're in an acting class and the teacher has asked you to play out a scene in which the only two players are you and Freddy Kruger! You look in a mirror and gradually allow fear to build up, with wide eyes, a racing pulse and rapid breathing until you let out a scream. Make sure the neighbours can't hear or they'll probably come running.

Chapter 7

Smoking away those feelings

We're spending time on the emotions because one of the principal uses of smoking is to avoid feelings. If this is recognised, smoking can be used to get back in touch with our natural feelings. Let's take a look at some specifics.

Those of you who've spent time in poor countries will be aware of the beautiful smiles on the faces of the children. Providing the kids have sufficient to eat and the community is not ravaged by war, the poorer the community, the happier their kids (and often the grown ups). Why?

Imagine that you're an exuberant five year old in a Western household. Here's a range of the likely consequences of your activity.

"Hey, pal, you've just smashed my one and only antique car! Can't you be a bit more careful! I've had that car since I was ten years old and look at it now!"

"Watch out for that drink. I don't want to have to clean the rug again!"

"Look at your hands. How many times must I tell you? Wash your hands before you touch the walls. Better still, keep your hands off the walls altogether!"

"Be quiet. I'm trying to watch this!"

Imagine the deep seated shame, guilt and sorrow induced in children by parental responses. It is estimated that the average five year old child receives about 400 "negative" messages and about 40 "positive" messages in any 24hr period. These common, everyday admonishments are repeated constantly throughout childhood. In a poor household, there's no antique car to smash, no carpet on which to spill a soda, no sodas to rot the teeth necessitating an expensive and irritated trip to the dentist, no television for siblings to squabble over, no parental frustrations at incomplete homework, no pristine walls from which loud screams reverberate in the tension filled recesses of parental brains, etc…

The child receives nowhere near as many parental criticisms and those he does receive are delivered with nowhere near as much emotional intensity. Apart from parents worrying about their possessions and their real estate, children are driven in many other ways. The more wealthy and developed a country the more parents invest in the success of their children, resulting in children who are stressed out by the time they're ten years old. No wonder some of them start smoking soon thereafter!

I can recall getting on a plane at Colombo airport in Sri Lanka after living in a fishing village in the south of the island for a few months. The plane was en route from London to Sydney and after the smiles of the village children, boarding a plane full of Westerners was like entering a morgue! In many Western cultures expressions of joy are repressed in children and almost forbidden in adults.

What has smoking got to do with this?

> **We often reach for a cigarette when we're really enjoying ourselves.**

One of the reasons for smoking is to curtail moments of uninhibited joy, to stop going "over the top" which is forbidden much of the time in our society. Smoking enables us to calm down a bit and still enjoy ourselves, but gives us a structured activity for a while. Group smoking includes everyone in the tribe and sets limits on any emotional "extravagances".

Smoking before, after (and occasionally during) sex is a common practice.

Human sexuality is the most rigidly proscribed of all human activity in many societies. Sex is so distorted by social mores, political, religious and gender politics that no-one has a clue what's "natural" any more. Too little energy for sex will result in a complaint of being too passive and without passion, whilst too exuberant an approach may result in allegations of insensitivity or even rape, at least for men. Women who engage in natural sex may be labelled deviant and driven from society, or worse.

Smoking smoothes these troubled waters, for it mitigates the criticism of a lack of passion by involving the parties in a "sexy" activity, and it blunts the full blown, frightening and much proscribed passion of a natural sexual being. Some sexual joy is socially acceptable, sexual abandon is not.

In addition, nicotine may prolong the "high" of sexual orgasm, and find itself in demand at this and other social occasions where people are freeing themselves from normal inhibitions. Smoking may alleviate the need for a more in depth interaction with others by providing a couple or group with a common activity. Embarrassment is reduced by shifting the focus from sex or uninhibited behaviour to the shared activity of smoking, itself a little risqué.

The emotion that smoking best alleviates is fear. Fear has many guises.

Many of us would say that we smoke to alleviate anxiety, which is another term for fear.

Often underlying our current anxieties is a belief that we're not good enough, that we don't deserve the unconditional love of parents, partners, others and ourselves, and that we're a fraud waiting to be exposed. Smoking gives us a degree of coolness and belonging, at least in groups where it isn't condemned. And in others, smoking affords notoriety. Some 15% of adults in the developed world smoke cigarettes and consumption is increasing in less developed nations.

We've noted that emotional expression is a vital component of mental and physical health.

We can use smoking to explore what we're feeling and what we're avoiding.

This exploration may reveal fears in our immediate lives and underlying fears that come from the past. We may be less aware of the old fears that emanate from not being cared for perfectly as children. Remember, no human beings are perfectly cared for. It isn't possible. If you had a response to that statement along the lines of, "I had a perfect childhood. My parents cared for me perfectly!" then you may be denying aspects of your childhood that are too painful to address, or trying to maintain an unrealistic view of life. Smoking helps keep you away from awareness until you're ready. Our unwillingness to care for ourselves now, and our unwillingness to stop criticising ourselves, is usually a reflection of a childhood that led us to believe that we weren't good enough.

If smoking alerts us to the need to care for ourselves better, it has made a major contribution to our health and well being.

Nicotine reduces the anxiety we feel as a consequence of not caring adequately for ourselves.

When you next light up become aware of what you're feeling and what you're uncomfortable with.

We know more of the origin of our emotions since we last tried this exercise. Remember the emotions are anger, sadness, fear and joy, plus a whole range of others that are made up of these basic feeling states. Which ones are problematic for you?

We talked about joy and fear. What about anger and sadness? Are they equally handled by smoking?

Sadness is an emotion that can be masked by the dynamism of youth. By the age of thirty however, it reasserts itself, and can then be seen etched into the face of a sufferer. It invariably has its origins in childhood. If some catastrophic life event at a later age causes us to be sad, it will pass after an appropriate time. If the sadness remains, it's not due to the event we believe has "caused" it, but is a response to left over, incomplete emotions from childhood. If we feel sad a lot of the time and for "no reason", we need to think about what happened in our lives before we were six years old.

Smoking takes the edge off sadness and gives us something to do.

Depression is commonly thought of as a deep sadness, but usually depression is an absence of any of the feeling states. If we express any of the emotions freely, it's difficult to be depressed at the same time.

An *angry* person may prefer to burn a cigarette, rather than experience the sensation of burning up inside.

An unpleasant incident may lend some urgency to lighting up in order to avoid the raw experience of anger and fear. These feelings may get so powerful as to necessitate not only immediate relief but longer term modification as well. Smoking suits perfectly.

A number of readers may have reached this point in this book and be thinking:

"None of this applies to me. I don't suppress my emotions and I don't criticise myself or others."

In this event, are there other reasons for continuing to smoke?

If, for example, you're smoking for purposes of social inclusion, i.e. all your mates smoke down the pub, and in order not to stand out, you join them, then ask yourself what it might mean for you if the other group members were to exclude you. There may be real situations where such exclusion may be more threatening to your well-being than any adverse health effects of smoking. The best course of action in that situation may well be to smoke.

It may be that you have no reasons to smoke, and none to not smoke. It might be that you simply "enjoy it". If so, keep reading.

Chapter 8

Habit and Addiction

Habits and addictions consist of actions, thoughts and feelings that cannot be abandoned without discomfort. Common usage defines an addiction as more powerful than a habit.

Habit or addiction is a matter of degree, but neither can be abandoned without some discomfort, and the principle emotion involved in the discomfort is fear. The habit must be preferable to its alternative in some way for it to become established, and as it continues, the reason for taking it up is forgotten. Fear of doing something differently, fear of the unknown and a fear of experiencing emotions replace the original fear, which may no longer be obvious.

Eventually the fear, usually recognised as anxiety, becomes associated with breaking the habit rather than what created it in the first place. We become anxious about changing our routine, afraid of change itself.

For example, we may have started smoking when we took on a more responsible job five years ago, and even though we now do the job with relative ease, we continue to smoke because of the anxiety associated with stopping the habit.

It's become politically expedient for the anti-smoking lobby to claim that nicotine is responsible for people becoming "addicted to cigarettes", but without the underlying pre-existing habits, few people would be susceptible to nicotine. The nicotine replaces the existing habits or addictions, rather than creating them.

Thinking, feeling and doing are all habit forming.

This realisation is vital to our mental and physical health.

The beliefs, "I'm not good enough", "I should be better", "I'm not up to it", and their immediate representations, "I'm not slim, pretty, smart, wealthy, sexy, romantic, tall, fast, strong, successful, organised, together, compassionate or friendly enough", are habits which cannot be broken without the unwanted side effect of fear, and may therefore be regarded as addictive.

Many of us would regard compulsive drinking, the frequent taking of uppers and downers, cocaine, cigarettes, prescription opioids, marijuana, antidepressants, heroin, coffee and slimming pills as addictions, but less inclined to regard our repeated self-analysis and self-criticisms in the same light.

And yet criticisms are at the heart of the substance addictions, all of which serve to avoid the more painful underlying core addiction.

No less addictive (and possibly more obnoxious to others) are the "positive judgements" which *we're in the **habit** of* making. "I know I'm right", "My kids are brought up better than that", "I know a good suburb when I see one", "I'm an excellent judge of character", "I have God on my side", "I pride myself on keeping a tight ship", " If you want it done properly you have to do it yourself", are all *judgements*. It doesn't matter whether the judgements are "good" or "bad". What matters is the intensity, the underlying fear with which they're held. Rigidity is the outcome. This unavailability for alternative views is the major addiction for most of us, brought up as we were by parents who struggled to make sense of life themselves. We have to be "right" to feel safe.

The determination with which we maintain our "rightness" also restricts our immune system and causes illness.

The "strength" of our convictions is determined by the depth of our underlying fear.

This is something upon which the anti-smoking lobby might dwell. There are so many people determined to be "right" about smoking, often abandoning all objectivity along the way, including scientific objectivity, that the degree of illness being created within themselves and the damage done to smokers may be exceeding any good which they may be doing. Surrounded by like, equally defended minds, the experience of criticising others to feel good about yourself is a very uplifting one, carried along on a wave of euphoria which serves to avoid one's usual self doubts. But how long does this last, especially when the subject of your zeal, the smoker, appears at least partially recalcitrant, unwilling or unable to see the benefit of your efforts to "help him"?

Extending unconditional acceptance to all human beings, whether they choose to smoke or not, cured more people of addiction than trying to persuade, cajole, beat, threaten, scare, assault or otherwise entice them to stop.

All thoughts, feelings and actions are a consequence of our personality, whose *habitual* pattern is to seek safety above all else. This craving for safety dictates our attitudes, opinions, beliefs, self-images and conclusions. We believe that there's something wrong with us, that we deserve to suffer for our imperfections and that the guilt we feel is justified. We end up having to protect ourselves from our own self criticisms. We then create an outside environment that similarly attacks us, and for protection from it, we double our defences and our addictions. ((

(Addiction = thoughts, feelings and actions unable to be dispensed of without discomfort = Fear)

We're addicted to self criticism, attack, and judgements of all kinds.

From our craving for safety comes our principal addiction…our personality.

The work we do, the food we eat, the movies we like, the sports we watch and play, our attractions, our child rearing *habits*, our sexual behaviour, the way we drive, our relationships, what we drink, the music we like, and a multitude of small, inconspicuous activities are all addictions. We don't regard many of them as such because they cause no problems, in fact they're helpful.

Our judgement of one thing as preferable to another is itself an addiction, because the act of judgement is an attempt to control, to make sense of, and to reduce to manageable proportions an unmanageable Universe.

All beliefs are no more than expediencies, the purpose of which is to keep our view narrow and manageable.

It makes sense of the intensity with which we defend our view and our opinions, even though on some level we understand them to be arbitrary. We defend them because the alternative is too difficult, which is to acknowledge that *we don't have a clue*, that all our opinions are entirely self-serving and not based upon any objectivity at all. A world in which we allowed all views an equal hearing would be unmanageable and alienate a tribe of people whose similar fictions, masquerading as unassailable facts, provide us with safety and membership of the tribe.

Hence the Catholic and Protestant youths who fight each other on the streets of Northern Ireland do so **not** because of a logically argued conviction of the ecclesiastical superiority of their religion, (they couldn't care less), but because of their need to belong to the tribe. Their belief in their particular religion is expedient but also expendable. Their membership of the tribe, on the other hand, keeps them alive. Tribes, for much of the period of human evolution were small, and belonging to them critical to survival in a hostile environment. We've not progressed much beyond this point emotionally, though technology has given us a "global society". The global society supports us financially and politically, but doesn't diminish the fear of *not belonging* which still dominates our "old brain" and dictates much of our behaviour. People capable of exploiting our need to belong provide the less discerning with mantras which make them acceptable to the tribe. Members are then forced to do the organisation's bidding under threat of expulsion should they allow common sense and propriety to contradict the self-inflicted delusions of the tribe.

The tribe of smokers

There are advantages to belonging to the tribe of smokers. Smoking is a readily identified marker, and in today's world of heavy criticism of smokers, creates a powerful, well defended, homogeneous group. The strength of the attack upon smokers unifies them and helps them over-ride a multitude of differences between the group's members.

The sometimes brutal assault by the anti-smoking lobby may be creating the opposite effect from that which was intended. Having ostracised a readily identifiable group in an increasingly homogeneous society, by continuing their stridency against smoking and smokers they drive people into the group. Their attempt to ban smoking everywhere is creating subterfuge.

One of the reasons why we try and make our world smaller is because of the nature of human biology. The child comes from the assured confines of the womb into an overwhelming world in which nothing can be taken for granted. The child struggles to narrow this world to a manageable state as quickly as possible, soaking up parental attitudes like a sponge and assigning them "fact" and "truth" status in order to facilitate the process.

All our addictions are addictions to the past.

Addictions avoid the present.

Being present is so remote from most people's everyday experience that few of us can understand it, let alone *be* it. Being present means allowing all thoughts, emotions, bodily sensations and actions to occur without grasping at some and trying to avoid others. We allow life to dictate our experience rather than desperately trying to control it. Some of us pay lip service to this but few of us are prepared to experience the fear it inevitably creates.

Cigarette smoking, like all addictions, avoids *being*.

Smoking gives us something to do, to feel, to think even, rather than experience... being.

The experience of *being* is sometimes likened to the experience of "nothingness".

Smoking surrounds us with a haze through which we can observe life, at a distance, bending reality to suit our need for safety above any other experience.

Lets take a look into that world between our "reality" and the experience of "being".

Would you like to try a very simple experiment?

Place the tip of your right index finger upon the tip of your nose.

Notice anything whilst you were doing it?

Not much?

Now repeat the exercise, this time taking five minutes to do it. I'll wait...

Did you do it?

No?

I thought not.

Now come on, you can spare five minutes. Have another go…

(5 mins later)

What did you notice?

Perhaps you noticed the first muscle that came into action when you decided to move your arm. Was it a muscle in your hand, shoulder, back, hip, leg, foot…?

In your arm, you say. Hmmmm…Try the exercise again.

Or maybe you became fascinated by the fine corrective changes that you made every time your finger strayed off target, like the multiple corrections a spacecraft makes when docking at a space station.

Or did you notice your breathing? Or your mind chattering away?

Did you become uncomfortable? Was five minutes too long to be engaged in doing something that normally takes less than a second?

Maybe thoughts and feelings came rushing to your rescue to avoid any experience of the vacuum that the lack of *doing* exposed.

Did you want to hurry up? Was it peaceful? Did you feel a connection with yourself whilst you were doing it?

Maybe not this time.

What would it be like doing nothing for five minutes?

If you think this would be easy, have a go. It may feel like it's driving you mad after a very short period of time.

We're so busy doing things by habit that we rarely experiencing the here and now. Mostly we're occupied by thoughts from the past or about the future, and by feelings coming from some left over event, or perhaps anticipating something coming up.

"So what!" you say.

Being in the present means existing without the defences and adaptations which we acquired as children and maintain now as grown ups, out of fear. Those defences keep us cocooned within the protective perimeter of our personality, the filter through which we relate to the outside world and through which we distil and manipulate experience so that we remain comfortable. However, our defences also keep us away from nature and from being in communion with other people. They keep us safe on the one hand, but because they restrict our immune system, they guarantee illness on the other. Shedding them, even for brief moments, may open us up to healing possibilities both from within ourselves and from without. Our immune system and endocrine systems can get on with the work for which millions of years of evolution has equipped them, and can allow healing to reach us from our environment, from our Universe.

We allow nature to do its magic every moment of every day. Whenever we breathe, eat or drink, we allow natural phenomena to sustain us. Nobody "decides" to be short of breath, to be hungry or thirsty. Being present, being in the moment, being spontaneous, and allowing ourselves to simply be, allows the process of communion with nature to nurture us, unhindered by what we think, feel or do.

Which of the following options might facilitate healing?

Walking through a meadow smelling the perfume of the wild flowers whilst listening to the birds sing, or walking through the same meadow thinking of how to make more money? In the former you're available, in the latter, unavailable.

We need something to remind us to experience the present.

How about smoking!

When you next reach for a cigarette, will you allow your hand grasping the packet and then withdrawing the cigarette to remind you of taking a few moments to simply *be*.

This means *being*, without an agenda. You don't know what might happen. You don't know what should happen. You don't know what's best to happen. You're handing over the agenda to the Universe for a while.

Whatever thoughts arise, let them. They're not you.

Whatever emotions arise, let them. They're not you.

Whatever bodily sensations arise, let them. They're not you.

If you're not those things, then who are you?

Ah… who are you?

If smoking initiates an Inquiry into "Who am I?" it may prove a very valuable activity indeed.

Chapter 9

Breathing and Smoking

We interact with our world in many different ways.

On an obvious and mechanical level we take food, water, air and warmth into our bodies and we discharge waste back into our surroundings. A cycle of involvement with our world is happening continuously and without it we wouldn't survive, literally for a second. If the warmth of the sun were lost, we'd snap freeze. Without air we'd die in a few minutes and survive water and food deprivation only marginally longer. We're given life by our surroundings in ways we rarely think about.

None of this stops us believing that we're in control however!

We don't have to create a favourable environment, we've been given it. We do have to manage it.

Our very existence is granted us, and once born, nature keeps us alive. We don't have to do anything. We don't have to work out how to be born, how to grow, how to heal ourselves and how to die. It just happens. We most effectively fulfil our role by letting our world evolve, part of which it does through us. The individual ways in which we witness life unfolding are our contributions. No two will be the same and no one is better than any other.

Breathing is perhaps the most immediate way in which we interact with our surroundings. Approximately twelve times a minute we breathe in our world, then we let go, and the Universe breathes us out. We breathe in using our nervous and muscular systems, automatically and out of our awareness, but we passively expire as gravity forces air from our lungs and back into the atmosphere. Of course we can over-ride automatic respiration, consciously increasing or decreasing our respiratory rate. For a couple of minutes we can even stop breathing altogether. Then we're forced to breathe again whether we like it or not.

Think about our breathing for a moment.

This vast Universe of which we know so little is breathing this tiny little organism we call a Human Being. It breathes through us. We are the breath of that Universe. So too are the trees, flowers, animals and all living things. Are there any things that aren't breathing? Perhaps a rock, although it's certainly interacting with its surroundings, and may even be breathing very, very quietly.

All matter continually builds up and breaks down. All matter is in a state of interaction with its surroundings. Inestimable numbers of particles stream across the boundaries of all matter, "living" or otherwise, every second. We're in an ongoing dance or interaction with all creatures, all things and the Universe. We're part of creation and our surroundings in a way that gave us life and sustains our life, whether we acknowledge it or not and whether we imagine that we're separate from it or not. We exist as a part of all those things we believe are outside of us, and with which we usually don't identify. Trillions of micro-organisms cover the surface of our body and colonize our intestine. They interact with our mind and our body. We can't survive without them.

Chaos and calm, peace and war, flowers and nettles, love and bitterness, the beautiful and the ugly, the enlightened master and the murderer. All are part of us.

The acceptance of the parts we like and those we don't, makes us whole.

If life scares us in some way and we're not prepared to trust it, we try and modify it. This means modifying us as well as our interaction with life. We want to deny some of it. We want it to be as we say it *should* be. We want it to suit us. We want to control life, us, and our responses to life. Needs arise in childhood, and we maintain them out of fear, as adults.

As kids, the more we could control life, the safer we felt. By learning to control life we believed that we'd stay approved of, and alive. At least that's what we figured, and this was reinforced by mum and dad who lived as though life was unsafe in some way and who implied by their actions that the struggle for control was paramount.

Our attitudes, beliefs, opinions and things of which we claim *we're certain* are all attempts to filter life through our own self-serving reality, for safety. We do things, think things and feel things in order to maintain that reality and stay feeling safe.

Smoking modifies our Universe in a fundamental way.

Smoking inserts a filter between us and our Universe, between us and life.

Instead of allowing our body physiology to breathe in, and atmospheric pressure to breathe us out, we modify this interaction by inserting a cigarette into the loop.

Why?

Because we don't want life to breathe us. We're not ready.

So between us and the Universe we insert a tube of tobacco, and by the time the air has reached us we've modified it, controlled it. We burn the tobacco, make the air smoky, less pure, less clear.

We don't like the clarity of existence without the illusions. This is the case whether we smoke or not, and one of the advantages of smoking is that other illusions we create need not be as profound.

Smoking has removed the fear of being present.

Smoking affords us the luxury of circumspection.

This is why some smokers have an edge of reality to them which is somewhat difficult to define, and un-nerves some non-smokers. The smoking permits them to be different because it takes care of at least some of the unknown, reducing some of the fear associated with being different.

We need to temper life, reduce it to the manageable, so we warm up the air, make it cloudy and speed it through a narrow opening into our lungs. We confine the point of entry into our bodies. We avoid breathing in breadth. We're not happy with air entering us in a way dictated by life so we bring it under our control. By doing this we hope to stay safe, and as we've previously discussed, avoid unwanted emotions, thoughts and realisations.

All of us are scared to some degree, though often the basis of our fear is unknown to us. We may recognise it as a discomfort, perhaps loneliness, a feeling of not quite belonging, a slight ongoing irritation, anxiety or disaffection with life.

We don't trust life and we attempt to exert control over it.

We become addicted to the methods of control.

Let's experiment with taking in a slice of unadulterated life.

Our role in this exercise is to allow ourself to be breathed, to take a breath of air in and allow gravity to breathe us out. For this exercise we need to become aware of some habit of ours. Anything which is recurrent and which annoys us, will do.

This may be a physical habit like smoking, jogging, drinking coffee or masturbating; an emotional habit like getting angry with someone at work, being scared of exams; or a habit of thought, such as always thinking that people aren't noticing us, or thinking poorly of us. We'll recognise this habit from the voice in our heads which constantly reminds us of our shortcomings (or superiority), whether we ask for its opinion or not!

Allow the next time you recognise a habitual pattern of yours to initiate this exercise.

Allow yourself to be breathed by your Universe. Become available to be breathed, without helping and without getting in the way. Allow an unadulterated interaction with life.

We don't know what will happen if we do this, because it's an exploration. We take a risk and we take our time taking it.

Allow yourself to be breathed for a while.

Chapter 10

Smoking with Love

What is love?

When we attempt to define love we usually resort to associating it with things which we say are good. Bad things are not associated with love, although the expression "tough love" in respect of certain childrearing practices has recently gained favour.

Of course it's our ego which is judging whether or not something is good or bad. Recall our ego is the accumulation of past experiences made up of beliefs, attitudes, opinions and anything we believe to be "true". Our personality is another term for it.

We might say that rescuing someone is an act of love and injuring someone is not, caring for someone is loving, attacking him or her is not. Being pleasant is loving, being rude isn't; a beautiful child is lovely, a rubbish tip is not. Good things are associated with love and bad or ugly things are what love is not.

By judging things as good or bad our ego guarantees its ongoing relevance and existence.

Our ego keeps us from experiencing love to its fullest, but at the same time it keeps us safe. All our judgements, interpretations, opinions and answers arise from the same desperation for safety. What we deem to be good or bad is therefore only a reflection of what we believe to be best for us.

Were we able to put aside our primary need for safety, our judgement of what's good and bad would be different, in fact it would cease to exist.

Everyone sees good and bad differently because we all have different needs and our pronouncement of good and bad is not objective, but self serving. Ask the child scavenging for his existence on a rubbish dump in the Philippines if rubbish dumps are better than a vase of beautiful flowers. Our judgement of good and bad applies as much to pronouncements about smoking, either declaring smoking to be good or bad, as it does to every other pronouncement made by any of us.

All our opinions are self serving.

They serve to maintain our defence system and give us a feeling of safety. They enable us to belong to a tribe and to make an otherwise overwhelming world, manageable.

Every thought in our head is in this category, it doesn't matter what it is, good or bad. It was put in our head by a set of circumstances when we were young. We judge ourselves and others, positively and negatively, not because there's any truth in our pronouncements, but because the very act of pronouncement keeps us safe. The alternative is to acknowledge that our experience covers but a fraction of possible experience and in the broader context, we're simply unable to say anything sensible about anything. Knowing nothing is not highly prized in most societies.

Let's become a little more familiar with our own judgements.

The first step is to acknowledge that we're incapable of listening without prejudice.

None of you is listening to what I'm saying, (I'm not suggesting that you do…☺) You're listening to what you're saying about what I'm saying.

We filter what we read through our pre-existing belief systems and respond with a hybrid thought consisting of someone else's comments, bent to fit our prejudices.

Many experiments have shown that if an identical passage is given to a group of people to read, there will be as many interpretations of the passage as you have people reading it, especially if the content is emotive.

Our ego edits, sanitizes, makes palatable and plain ignores anything it judges to be not in the interests of maintaining safety, i.e. maintaining itself. No film censor is as innovative or as judgemental, for the ego always chooses suffering ahead of freedom, for freedom decommissions the ego.

The ego or personality is the protective perimeter in which we cocoon ourselves and through which we filter nature. Because we attack ourselves, attack others, and invite attack from the outside, we can justify the need for our defences.

If we attack ourselves less, we invite less attack from outside and we require fewer defences, therefore enabling us to drop at least a few of our prejudices and let at least a little of the outside world in. As we listen less to the voice in our own heads running its constant commentary, we become available to actually listen.

The trick then, is to allow the thoughts in our heads to be there, without assigning reality or truth to them. This lets them co-exist with new thoughts without dominating them. Eventually they decommission themselves, since they exist in the service of a set of conditions that no longer exist, i.e. our past conditioning, and we've moved on from that.

"What was that?" we enquire of the voice in our heads.

"You really blew that, dummy!"

"Why, thank you. I appreciate you dropping by and giving me your opinion. It must be at least five minutes since you last came by. I was beginning to think I'd lost you", we reply in good humour.

We don't need to fight our ego. We acquired it for safety and it's served us well. We can make friends with it, joke with it, come to love it.

Ultimately we come to recognise that we don't actually create our own thoughts. Had anyone else been through our set of life circumstances that person would be visited by the same set of thoughts as us. In that sense our upbringing and our culture are "thinking us".

We're being thought by our past attitudes, beliefs and opinions.

Damn it, we're being "thunk"!

Just recognising that our "reality" is really a bunch of left over thoughts, most of which are well past their "use by date", frees us from being controlled by them. They have served us well, but the next stage of our liberation in life requires that we move on from these restraints. We're like a tree that's been staked as a sapling. The stake protects the tree against the elements, but eventually, if it's to grow to its full potential, the very thing which kept it alive must be removed. Another example of needing to eventually let go to fulfil our potential is that of a space rocket. The payload needs the large rockets to get it out of the Earth's gravitational pull. As soon as the rockets have achieved that goal, they must be discarded if the payload is ever to make outer space.

The need for judgement, to be certain of what's good and bad, what's right and wrong, starts to give way to another way of being……acceptance. When acceptance shows up, love is not far behind.

We start to see love everywhere. All thoughts, feelings and actions, whatever they are, contribute to learning about us and our world. They're all part of what love is.

When we start saying what's good and bad, we don't feel love. Love hasn't gone away, for it cannot go away. It is however, temporarily concealed by our need for safety.

Smoking needs to be looked at in this way. It isn't good or bad, right or wrong. It has been part of our method of survival and continues to be as long as we smoke.

Smoking is part of our survival and part of our quest for love.

Nothing could be more honourable.

Smoking, criticising ourselves for smoking, criticising others for smoking, concern with smoking, wanting to give up smoking, giving up smoking, taking up smoking and any other activity associated with smoking are all vehicles for exploring love, perhaps ultimately the only worthwhile human pursuit.

Love may be regarded as evolutionary. Each individual has his own evolutionary path to walk, for this guarantees the survival of the species. The Universe never stops changing, and we must change with it. Love is the way whereby we connect with that Universe and all others in it. It is the common fabric that co-ordinates and unifies evolution. Every creature plays its part.

Smoking, like any other habit, can be used to destroy you, or move you towards love.

If you've gotten this far with this book, the likelihood is that you're exploring letting love into your life.

This exploration takes time.

We start to explore loving ourselves, caring for ourselves, trusting ourselves, acknowledging ourselves, respecting ourselves and accepting ourselves in a way in which we hoped that others would, and they didn't. We hoped our parents would love us perfectly, and they didn't. They did the best job they could but ultimately, love needs to be explored by taking responsibility for it ourselves and not expecting others, with their own needs, to do it for us. No-one can take responsibility for us feeling love even if that is their intention, for love by another eventually irritates us if we aren't loving of ourselves.

Perfect love on planet Earth is a rare state.

We can explore loving ourselves for who we are now, not for whom we may become, and if we need to smoke now, then smoking becomes part of what we love.

Chapter 11

Becoming aware of criticisms

It's hard to imagine a little child feeling loved if she's being constantly criticised.

One of the first steps in allowing love back into our lives is to become aware of the criticisms we make of ourselves, or, if we're in the habit of sparing ourselves criticism, become aware of how we criticise others. We've said before that these two things are essentially the same. The criticisms become a habit or an addiction, requiring a bolstering of defences and a refusal to admit any new realisations. They keep us safe but they keep us unfulfilled. Smoking may serve a similar function. Neither should be dispensed with lightly.

When it comes to self-criticism we can use the model of the Grown Up and the Little Kid. The Grown Up is that part of us which is both nurturing of the Little Kid and critical of him or her. The critical part is called the Critical Parent and the nurturing part the Natural Parent. The Little Kid is the repository of adaptations from childhood, the so called Adapted Child, and the spontaneous free part of the child is called the Free Child. The Grown Up and the Little Kid relate to each other within the individual pretty much like we adults relate to our real children, sometimes critical, sometimes nurturing.

The following scenario helps us understand the consequences of self-criticism.

Pick something of which you're critical. It might be something simple, like "I'm fat", or more complex like "I can never make up my mind". When you've come up with something, proceed with the following exercise.

Imagine that you and another person are watching a group of children play. The kids are between three and six years old. You have a pretty good idea what the kids are like after watching them for half an hour or so. They stop playing and leave, all except this little boy or girl (pick one the same sex as yourself) who approaches the two grown ups and ignoring the person with you, takes you by the hand. This child is about four years old.

Imagine that this kid is with you now. Which hand is he holding?

The other grown up approaches, ignores you, and says to the four year old in a critical tone.

"I've been watching you play now for some time and I can't help noticing how fat you are (use your own self-criticism) compared with the other kids. I mean look at them. They've all got lovely neat little bodies. Not like you. What's the matter with you! Can't you do something about it? You must be really weak. I've seen a gnat with more will power than you!"
With this the critical grown up departs, leaving you holding the hand of a trembling, distraught four year old.

What do you do?

Go ahead, imagine that you're there now.

The likelihood is that you'll bend down to the child and comfort him or her, whilst probably telling the critical stranger to beat it.

"There, there, he was a horrible man wasn't he. And what would he know? I think that you're gorgeous. I wish I had a bit more padding to cover these old bones of mine. Can I have some of yours do you think….."

With a bit of a cuddle and a tickle of the child's tubbiness, you reassure her that she's wonderful and loveable, just as she is.

This distraught child represents you. The little child who still resides inside us all, waiting for the day when a parent figure (we usually cast our partner in the role) will come along and make up for all the hurts of childhood. When we criticise ourselves, we're not only refusing to go to the distraught child and comfort her, but we're criticising her instead.

The only person the child within us can ever expect to be there for her is her greatest critic. Now how do you think such a child would feel?

The answer to that is that the child would feel like you feel every time you criticise yourself or set yourself up to be criticised by others. Or if your habit is to criticise others instead of yourself, you may find yourself joining in with a crowd criticising someone else in order to avoid the scrutiny off yourself, a way to deny your own self-criticism. This may make you feel guilty, remorseful, angry and sad. Perhaps like a fraud.

All these circumstances arise from criticism of self and others.

Whenever you become aware of criticising yourself or others, imagine you have a little boy or girl with you, take that child by the hand and say,

"Sorry sweetheart. I take that back"

Of course you'll be tempted to say, "Damn. There I go again. Criticising myself!"

Which is criticising yourself for criticising yourself. So be gentle with yourself.

You're human, so you're critical. It's that simple.

The criticisms don't stop overnight, and nor should they, but they eventually become background noise. You're not trying to "get rid of them". You're recognising them, perhaps identifying where they come from, acknowledging them and even welcoming them.

Then they disappear in the same way they appeared. Without intervention by you.

Have fun with this. This little child will be delighted that the big person in his life has eventually found the time to spend with him, and is beginning to learn to be less critical. Those of you with your own children will know that children are incredibly loving and forgiving of parental inadequacies. Once again, take your time.

Chapter 12

Being a Smoker

Most of us are familiar with trying to *do* something about smoking, either taking it up, lighting up or giving it up.

Very few of us have any experience of *being* a smoker.

When it comes to smoking, many of us will have worried about it, tried to stop it, defended it, attacked it, taken it up, given it up, taken it up again, and perhaps become resigned to it. All of these things are in the *doing* category.

Have you discovered that trying to *do* something about a problem often doesn't seem to work? (I'll stop these annoying bold italics soon). Not long after we give something up, we take up something else as a substitute, or revert to the original addiction. We might take up smoking again, having given it up, or put weight back on not long after we take a whole load off. Why? We've done the hard part surely. It seems self destructive to just throw all that hard work away. And it is hard work. Anyone who's stopped smoking will be aware that it isn't easy.

The former smoker may take up cooking, reading, work, squash, travelling, public speaking or jogging, all of which may serve to avoid being with himself in a way not dissimilar to the smoking, if he's ***doing*** these distractions, and not ***being*** them. If, on the other hand we were to use any of these activities to explore *being* in our life, they'd be beneficial. As would smoking.

Health and well being may not be so much a matter of what we <u>*do*</u>, but a matter of how we <u>*are*</u>.

If something bothers us, we are exhorted by ourselves and other to ***do*** something about it, whereas the solution to the problem may be to ***be*** with it.

This idea takes quite a lot of digesting, so don't be too concerned if it makes little sense to you at this point in time. People come in various states of readiness to explore, and no state is preferable.

If we could work out a way of being present to the problem, we may not have to find a solution because being present to the problem may resolve it.

I know what you're thinking.

"That's great. But how do I ***do*** that?"

See how all pervasive the need to ***do*** is? (I know, I promised to can the bold font...)

The first step is to explore the difference between trying to achieve something, and *being*. Trying to achieve something implies the following:

1. There *is* a preferable method
2. There *is* a preferred outcome
3. You can *do* it.

These common assumptions may not be correct.

Being may be something that arises in the course of not attempting to do anything about a problem other than experience being with the problem. So what does *being* involve?

The human organism is active in several ways. Perhaps the most identifiable are:

1. Thinking
2. Feeling
3. Doing

We've spoken earlier about the need to express ourselves freely and the advantages to health from responding with a full range of emotions. Thinking has been mentioned in reference to the voice in our heads that continues to criticise us and keeps us safe by avoiding the unknown. And doing has been mentioned in connection with its use in avoiding being.

What areas of exploration might reveal the nature of being?

Judgement inhibits being.

As long as we continue to insist that one thing is right and another wrong, that one thing is good and another bad, we will continue to avoid being. It seems to us obvious which thing is good and which is bad, but all judgements are made at a point in time that no longer exists. They're superseded the moment they're made.

Missing out on a job today was *bad*. Tomorrow we're offered a better one and now missing out on yesterday's job is *good*, not bad. Being spurned by a love interest is *bad* until it frees us to meet someone we're more compatible with and now it's *good*. If we're prepared to experience the emotions of the thing we're calling bad, and those emotions are generally anger, sadness and fear, the judgement of the event being good or bad disappears.

The willingness to experience emotions, thoughts and actions without judging them is the experience of being.

Of course, judgement isn't easy to disengage. In practice the experience of emotions, thoughts and actions takes place in the presence of judgement followed by an awareness of judgement. At this stage both spontaneity and awareness of judgement are co-existing. Eventually the judgement disappears in the same way it came – of its own accord.

To enter into a different relationship with our thoughts is the first step in letting go of judgement, since much of the time the thoughts are themselves judgemental, and in addition, we treat many of the thoughts as though they're real and true, or as if they *are* us.

Chapter 13

Thinking about Smoking

A thought is a response to a stimulus.

An emotion is also a response to a stimulus, and much of the time the thoughts and emotions will be linked. Emotions may be regarded as a hormonal response to the neuronal discharges that constitute a thought. In that sense thoughts and emotions are the body's method of expressing the same response to the same stimulus using different parts of the body's physiology. Thoughts and emotions exercise the body physiology, like running exercises the musculoskeletal system, keeping it healthy.

Actions are also responses to stimuli using yet another part of the physiology.

We need to get into a different relationship with our thoughts in order to experience *being* with them.

***Being* with an issue might resolve it without needing to *do* anything about it.**

How does this apply to thinking? Firstly, we need to become aware that we're actually thinking.

Most of the time we don't hear voices in our head and we don't analyse our thoughts. We have no part of us monitoring our thoughts and so we go through life with our thoughts dictating reality without us being aware that this is happening. We rarely realise that what we believe may not be true. A thought is often generated by present circumstances invoking past events, and therefore its conclusions may be irrelevant or out of date. In the common vernacular, a "knee jerk" response. Perhaps a "neurone jerk" would be a more appropriate term.

Thoughts are a response to a stimulus, which, if the stimulus is external, will be registered by one of the five senses. Or the thought might be triggered by a bodily sensation.

For example:

External input, this time a statement: "Chocolate's non fattening" (stimulus)

"Rubbish!" (response).

Another statement from an external source: "Yoga's great" (stimulus)

"Yes, I love it" (response)

Oh….you didn't have that response! Well, that brings us to our next realisation. No two responses are the same to the same stimulus.

Why?

Doesn't everyone know that chocolate's fattening!

No, because some people eat chocolate and don't get fat. Their experience and therefore their response to the stimulus is different.

It's our experience, our childhoods and perhaps our genes that determine our response.

The stimulus comes from either outside of ourselves, as in the example above, or from within, such as a bodily sensation. We get a pain in our stomach and according to past experience, our response ranges from "What's that?" (no previous experience) to "Hell no!" (someone who's battled stomach ulcers all his life). Whether the stimulus is from outside or inside, once again, everybody's response is different.

If everyone's response is different, itself a consequence of no two lives having been exactly the same, then how can one judge one response to be "truer", one thought more representative of "reality", than another? Obviously, we can't. We can say that given a fixed set of circumstances our experience was X, but those circumstances have gone.

What's more, we don't determine the stimulus.

A thought is a response dictated by external circumstances not obviously under our control, or internal bodily sensations also not under our control.

A thought is an uncontrolled response to an uncontrolled stimulus.

No wonder we try and keep life under control when it so obviously isn't. And no wonder we try and convince ourselves that we "know", when we so obviously don't.

If thoughts are so out of our control, it might be better regarding them as not belonging to us at all. Sure, our mind is conveying or relaying the thought; "having" it if you like, and our mind is supplying the neurones and the neurotransmitters which make the thought, and it's our experience stored in our brains which respond to the external or internal stimulus, but none of that is *creating* the thought.

The thought is created when a set of present day circumstances comes into contact with a set of past conditions stored in our physical and psychological memory.

Imagine a biological organism, us, walking through the landscape of our own life. We didn't create ourselves and we didn't create the landscape. We represent the journey we've been through, our unique path through the landscape, influenced by a unique set of factors. We find ourselves at a point in place and time, neither determined by us. Our five senses, seeing, hearing, touching, smelling and tasting monitor the external circumstances. The stimulus from outside of us meets the accumulated experience (memory) stored within us and generates a response from the biological organism. The response consists of thoughts, feelings, bodily sensations and actions.

Memory is both psychological, the memory we usually identify with, as well as body memory, a set of physiological responses the body has previously undergone and whose remnants remain, stored within the muscles and internal organs.

We are an organism created by the Universe. We had no say in our creation nor our fifteen million years of evolution. We respond to circumstances created by the Universe and our responses are dictated by a past over which we had no control.

Instead of regarding our thoughts as our own it may be more accurate to see them as one of the many functions of our Universe.

The Universe is thinking through an agent of itself…us.

The Universe is thinking us.

We are being thought by the Universe.

We're being thunk!

It may be very difficult to move beyond our old adaptations, our old problems and our old addictions if we never address the matter of our thoughts, where they're coming from and who or what they belong to.

Why?

The struggle to change thoughts from "negative" to "positive" meets with universal failure. We try and convince ourselves that if we repeat something frequently enough long enough, we'll actually start to "believe" the positive thought. However, experience suggests that this doesn't happen, and the above explanation of the nature of thoughts explains why.

Affirmations are an attempt to control the uncontrollable.

How can we achieve some peace from the constant haranguing or the repetitious criticism of our thoughts? That criticism may be "good" or "bad", affirming or negating.

What might result from not attempting to change our thoughts?

You can't change them anyway, for they're not yours to change.
Accepting our thoughts, whatever they are, however critical or congratulatory, progresses them from being regarded as a "truth" which runs us, to being regarded as visitors espousing but one of a multitude of possibilities. Other people's thoughts and opinions represent yet more perspectives.

Our thoughts are the consequence of a collision of past and present circumstances and indicate the journey of one member of the human family through life thus far.

As with a library which tries to maintain a faithful record of history up to present time and would not suffer someone trying to change that history after the event, thoughts are a faithful representation of our journey thus far and do not stand being changed. There's no need anyway to change them. They are only worrisome when we fail to recognise what they really are, and relate to them as though they're the irrefutable truth. There's another component of not recognising the nature of thoughts which troubles us all.

We **I**-dentify with our thoughts. This means that we fail to distinguish between our thoughts and our selves. Take the following example.

A man believes that he's aggressive. His father was aggressive and when our man was a boy his mother and aunt would discuss his father in very unflattering terms. Whenever he feels aggressive as a grown up he thinks, "I'm malicious". Since he fails to distinguish between his thought "I'm malicious" and himself, he believes that he's evil. He doesn't recognise that he's being visited by a thought guaranteed by the collision of his past conditioning and his current circumstances. What has this to do with him actually being evil…not much…nothing maybe?

The problem with thoughts is not their actual content, but that we identify with them.

We say they *are* us. That's the problem with them.

If our aggressive man comes to understand that his thoughts are not him, he may free himself from the feelings of sadness, despair and self-loathing which accompany his opinion.

Let's look at some thoughts related to smoking.

"I'm really hopeless", "I'm weak", "Ah, it's not a problem", "The bronchitis was here *before* I started smoking", "I'll stop one day", "Smoking is the only pleasure I have in life", "Smoking relaxes me like nothing else can", "If I stopped smoking I'd be laughed out of the group", and "It's a filthy habit" are problematic only if we identify with them.

We need to become an observer of our thoughts rather than their victim and controlled by them. We can't control them but they needn't control us either.

We become an observer, a witness to our thoughts by accepting them and by welcoming them. They give us an indication of where we've been and assist us in where we're going. We can celebrate them.

The next time you become aware of any conversation in your head or with another person about smoking, allow yourself to recognise that you're thinking, or that you're being thunk.

In the early days of practising this exercise you'll only identify the occasional thought. Most will get by you without you realising that you've been thunk.

You'll need some help.

Put up several signs around your house which say:

"I'm being thunk!"

If you're a smoker, you can light up a cigarette and listen to the thoughts that come racing into your mind.

"Thank you for visiting", you say, welcoming the thoughts, "I appreciate you calling".

Chapter 14

Accepting Smoking

The premise behind acceptance is simple. Learn to accept yourself, including everything you find it necessary to do and everything you've done, and you free yourself from the chains of self-criticism and self doubt. Anything that you're currently doing for the purpose of criticising yourself, will fall by the wayside.

Accepting yourself involves everything, not just some aspects of yourself that you or others judge to be *acceptable*. You can't accept yourself and continue to hold onto opinions about how bad some aspects of you or your behaviour are, hoping that by accepting the "good" things the "bad" things will somehow go away. They won't. They exist because of criticism and they're maintained by criticism.

You can't accept your sponsorship of an orphan from South East Asia and not accept your compulsive gambling; accept your weekly attendance at Church but not your smoking. You can't accept that you're a good father but not that you take prescription opioids. It doesn't work that way. Acceptance involves accepting everything.

Tell a few people that you've given up smoking and see what happens. Most likely they'll pat you on the back and congratulate you on your courage and common sense.

Now tell a few that you've accepted yourself as a smoker, and note their response. They'll most likely try and talk you into giving up.

Smoking provides the opportunity to practise acceptance.

In the act of acceptance, everything changes, as in the following:

Accept Everything

Change Nothing

and

Everything Changes

The act of refusing to accept something causes it to remain, as in the following.

Accept Nothing

try and

Change Everything

and

Nothing Changes

The very act of accepting smoking changes it.

Acceptance vs. Resignation

Acceptance is not resignation. Acceptance implies the willingness to experience the thoughts, emotions and the actions that accompany any experience. Resignation means remaining stuck in a situation with unresolved sadness and disappointment. All of us suffer disappointments and all of us experience sadness. These too will pass if acceptance is explored.

Being resigned to smoking is not healthy, for the organism remains confined by unfinished business and unable to use its full powers of protection and recovery. Being resigned to anything, is similarly unhealthy.

Acceptance of smoking transforms the act of smoking from an addiction to a pastime.

Smoking with acceptance has different effects to smoking with resignat

When you next light up, try this exercise.

Allow yourself to be as present as you can to any thoughts, feelings, actions or bodily sensations that arise.

If you're a person who attacks smokers, allow all your thoughts and feelings, criticisms, rage, as well as your thoughts and feelings of wanting to help smokers, to arise in the course of this exercise. Allow the next time someone near you lights up to initiate the exercise. Caring for the well being of smokers got many people involved in anti-smoking campaigns. Over time this natural care my have been replaced by the need to exercise control over other people's lives. Stridency and punitive action may have been the result.

Be as present and as accepting as you can to everything about the process. This takes time and cannot be rushed. Don't deny any of it. Be aware of your judgements.

To move beyond the thoughts, feelings and habits all you need to do is own them, be present to them and realise at the same time that they aren't you.

Throw a little love into the equation and before you know it you'll be embracing them.

They won't be back anytime soon.

Chapter 15

Loving the Smoker

Sometimes when we look in the mirror and see our ageing faces and battle worn expressions we find it a bit difficult experiencing much appreciation of ourselves, let alone loving ourselves. And yet self-love is the basis of recovery from any experience in life and the basis of moving along from any habit or addiction. Self love does not mean self congratulation. Self love is what happens when we experience being. In a literal sense it is "being…. in love".

One method of approaching the exploration of loving ourselves is to imagine that we're made up of the Grown Up part of us, which is the part staring back at us from the mirror, and the Little Kid in us, that part which continues to dominate our emotional life. The Little Kid represents the spontaneous, fun loving and loving part of us that got slowly whittled away during the course of living our lives. His fun and aliveness have gradually been replaced with a cynicism of life and a criticism of ourselves and others. Within the Little Kid is also the spontaneous expression of anger, sadness and fear, as well as joy.

If you have any need for this book to make a difference to you, either to your life, your smoking, or any other unwanted habit or addiction, then allow yourself to proceed with getting in touch with the Little Kid inside you, despite your cynicisms and your misgivings. After all, who's going to know?

Everyone, that's who!

When you turn up for work on Monday having been in touch with the Little Kid inside you, expect someone at work to say…

"My…what's different about you? You seem so much lighter."

"Oh, yeah…I had a good weekend. Does it show?" you reply.

If the Grown Up (the person we are now) is prepared to love and nurture the Little Kid (the essence of who we were as a child) in us, the Grown Up receives back unconditional love from the Little Kid. Unconditional love is the love only children seem capable of giving. They don't love us because of our money, status, looks, whether we smoke or not, our car, house, relationships or whatever. Little children open our hearts, and perhaps that's what the expression "Only we can open our own hearts" means.

Children love us as we are.

The love of the Little Kid is the love of us by ourself, i.e. self love. The child within us gets to feel safe and we get to feel loved.

When we feel the safety of self love we can let go of some of the defences, adaptations, addictions, beliefs and opinions and some of the diseases we developed when we needed to defend ourselves. We no longer need them. As a result of the feelings of security and love we experience when we let the Little Kid back into our lives we begin to relate to others in a much more open, caring and less defensive way.

How might we facilitate this evolution, remembering that it needs to be allowed to happen rather than being forced to happen? We've seen that we need do nothing different to attract caring, but continue to explore accepting ourselves exactly as we are now.
Lives are so busy these days that nobody has any time to do any reflection, and the notion of spending time with oneself is relegated to the bottom of the *must do* list.
To accept ourselves, we may need to become aware of the relationship we have with our own Little Kid, which, for most of us, is no relationship at all that we're aware of. The relationship which we're about to explore needs to be allowed to evolve. This is an ongoing process, not something achieved overnight, in fact, not something *achieved* at all. It happens in its own good time, much to our annoyance and frustration at times.

As we become available for the relationship to develop, nature takes over. As we accept the relationship between the Grown Up and the Little Kid in us, the relationship evolves.
Everything around us is evolving. Nothing stays the same for long, for evolution is part of nature. We don't have to

know how to grow and mature, for nature has determined it for us during fifteen million years of evolution.

The caterpillar turns into a butterfly not by learning how to do it, not by trying to do it, but by being a caterpillar.

To find out what your relationship is with yourself imagine that you have a little boy or girl in your care. Make the child the same gender as yourself. This little boy or girl is you. We can get some focus on our little person by checking out some photos of yourself as a child, or, if you're like me and born before the invention of the camera (just a little self effacing joke), you can use photos of your own children or anyone else's kids for that matter. Failing getting hold of any photos, use your imagination, the photos in your head.

Imagine that you're looking after your own Little Kid.

Whatever we might do with a real child we can do with our own Little Kids, except that we're in the luxurious position of being able to do as we would normally do and at the same time be accompanied by our Kids. Our exercise therefore takes little effort and no real time. Here are a few situations to get us started.

We might be working at our desk in the office or at home. We look over in the corner of the room and our Kid's working away at his own drawing.

"Hi, what's up", we enquire.

"I'm drawing a picture"

"Who's that?" we ask, leaning over to get a better look, "Daddy is it? Yeh, looks just like me."

Driving the car is a good time to dialogue with our Little Kids.

"Mummy. Who decided that I'd live with you?" or

"Daddy. Do birds have daddies too?" or, my favourite, actually asked by my own child when he was a four year old:

"Daddy. Why do I keep asking you "Why?" all the time?"

We carry on a conversation with the child as though a real child were there, building an appreciation of the relationship that we have with this child. Any other situation can be used to explore this relationship.

A friend of mine was enjoying his Little Boy when he accompanied him into a shop to buy a drink. The girl behind the counter asked him what he wanted.

"A Coke for me and an icecream for the Little Boy", he replied.

After unsuccessfully craning her neck to locate the little boy, she went to hand over the icecream. My friend paid for the goods, took the Coke and proceeded to leave without the icecream, still sitting in a holder on the counter.

"What about your icecream," the shop assistant called after him.

Turning to his Little Kid who was by this stage walking out of the shop with him, he replied, "Thanks, but he says that he doesn't want it now. He'll share my Coke instead".

Allow the exercise to be as much fun as being with kids can be.

If you're curled up watching TV imagine that the Little Boy or Little Girl is there with you. Or you might take a cuddly toy or pillow and carry it to a bed and put your Little Child to sleep. "Goodnight sweetheart", you say, giving your Little Child a big hug.

Hey, nobody else will know you're doing this, so be as outrageous as you like.

There will be times when you don't feel like looking after the Little Kid or you're angry with him.

"Why the hell should I look after you!" we may find ourselves shouting at him, "Nobody looked after me!"

All responses are equally valuable.

Some people report that they do the exercise for five minutes three times a day. Others say they remember the Little Kid twenty times a day for a few moments. Others forget the Little Kid altogether. There's no particular way in which you should be relating.

What you should be doing is what you are doing.

What you ought to have done is what you did.

What did you learn about the relationship between your Grown Up and your Little Kid?

Sometimes it's difficult to access loving feelings towards ourselves. It may be so long ago that we experienced love that we're out of practice. The following may help to re-acquaint you with tender feelings.

Select an object or a person whom you admire. You may even be prepared to say that you love him, her or it. It may be the tree outside your window, the painting on the wall, a small child, your partner, the sky, or a flower. Allow yourself to be in touch with the feelings you have for this person or object. Be as present to the loving feelings as possible, which may involve putting this book down for a few moments. Allow the feelings to well up inside, take you over if that's what happens. If they're barely there, that's also OK.

"Look at that gorgeous little boy", we may exclaim if we've chosen a little boy as the person we love or feel tender towards.

Now, try this.

Bring that feeling which you feel safe enough expressing back into yourself.

"I'm gorgeous"

"What a beautiful flower" may become "I'm a beautiful woman"

"I can really appreciate the workmanship in this table" becomes "I can appreciate myself."

We begin to identify with the expression of love, using something outside of ourself.

We allow the love of nature to initiate loving ourselves.

Sometimes we feel too uncomfortable directly acknowledging ourselves in this way. It may feel too phoney. You may be more comfortable imagining loving a small baby.

Imagine that you're cuddling a small baby in your arms. Take a pillow or soft toy and let yourself actually have the physical sensation of doing this. Let whatever feelings and thoughts arise. No need to analyse them. You may once again need to put the book down and let this happen over a period of time.

If you've come back to the book now, we need to use our powers of imagination for the next exercise.

Imagine that you're out walking on a clear, mild day.

You find yourself in an area that's vaguely familiar, though you're not sure why. You keep walking, past some houses, a park, some children, perhaps some shops, a parking lot, apartments or properties or open fields if you find yourself in the countryside. As you walk on, noting the roads and the surrounding areas, you begin to realise that you've been here before, for something about this area is quite familiar. You keep walking and slowly it dawns upon you that this is the area in which you lived when you were about five years old.

As you continue more memories return from your childhood. Other landmarks you recognise lead you down a familiar road and as you round a corner you see the house in which you and your family lived. You stand looking at it for a while, allowing the memory of it to return, and then slowly you approach the house. After a few moments you walk into the yard and up to the front door, which is open.

You look inside the house and notice a family that you recognise as your own family when you were a child. You see some grown ups which you know are your mum and dad or whoever was your caretakers. Perhaps there are some other kids there, your brothers and sisters, whom you also recognise.

As you watch and listen, you become aware of members of the family interacting with each other. Your concentration is suddenly broken by a small boy or girl coming into view whom you recognise as yourself. You watch the child interacting with the other family members for a while. In this child's face you see clearly the needs, fulfilments, angers, joys, fears, wants, losses and sorrows with which you're so familiar and with which you've lived all your life. They're obvious to you in a way no-one else in the family notices. You've not been struck before with the clarity of this realisation that your world is only really known to yourself. You notice what the child has to do in order to feel safe and to get what she or he wants in the family. He shows the strain of trying to work out how to best be in this family. She shows the anxiety of constantly seeking approval for who she is. Everything the child does or doesn't get for himself is clear as you continue to watch him.

The child senses he's being watched and turns to look at you.

Your eyes meet and you see within the child's face a look of recognition of who you are, a recognition from long ago, before the journey had almost begun. Both of you are absorbed in a moment devoid of all pretence.

Every part of the child's being is asking you a question which has led you to this moment and which you can no longer ignore. It's the only question of importance the child will ever ask you and it's asked with a profound love. The child is speaking to you....

"Will you look after me?"

"Will you care for me, cherish me and love me?"

Allow yourself to be with that question for as long as you need to be. Put down the book and come back to it later if you need to. There's no right answer to this question and no one, no one, not the child, nor me, nor anyone, will ever criticise your answer.

There's no point lying to the child, for he'll see it in an instant, and he'll know why.

If you're not ready to take responsibility for yourself right now, that's fine. That's how it should be. Your journey is a journey without time, without signposts and without a finishing line. There's no map and no lessons.

If the Universe had already travelled your path, you wouldn't be here.

If you're not ready to take care of yourself, tell the child.

"Sorry sweetheart. I'm not ready to give that undertaking just yet. But I won't be far away. I'll be here."

Children accept anything real, and are fooled by little that isn't.

Allow yourself to be with that Little Kid for a while, getting to know each other. He may take you on a tour of his house, a tour with which you're very familiar.

These exercises presume that the nature of love cannot be sensibly conveyed between humans using words.

Please accept my apologies for these clumsy efforts.

I don't know whether love can be created where there was none, but nature has a habit of doing the darndest things, given half the chance.

Chapter 16

Smoking as a problem

How long before we'll be happy?

What can I do to achieve unconditional love or enlightenment?

How can I love myself more?

How can I stop smoking?

How can I enjoy smoking without suffering any consequences?

We've been granted leave to explore these matters, if not resolve them. This period is called a lifetime.

Resolution occurs when we realise that nothing can be resolved by us, and our role is to explore and not resolve. The Universe resolves things, sooner or later. The overall design of life is utterly beyond us. That part of the brain capable of anything but a rudimentary understanding of the Universe is not yet sufficiently developed, in my view. We're only just beginning to comprehend the most basic sciences and observe the most obvious phenomena. The neuronal connections in our brain will expand to accommodate our new observations such that sensible interpretation of them will, in the future, become possible.

But right now, our theories are all we've got, and they reflect our primitive understandings using a part of the brain not yet capable of assimilating the facts.

Our need for resolution implies the presence of a problem.

Continuing to maintain that a problem exists for which a solution is required, guarantees the continuation of the problem, and the absence of a solution.

We cannot solve a problem using the framework within which we identify the problem, because the framework *is* the problem. Continuing to insist a problem exists maintains the framework and therefore the problem.

When we see the problem differently, it disappears.

As long as we see smoking as a problem, it's likely to persist.

When we no longer see it as a problem, the problem disappears.

Does this mean that if we no longer see smoking as a problem, we'll stop smoking?

The answer to that question cannot be known whilst smoking is still referred to as a problem and whist the notion of a problem requiring a solution is driving the question.

If we expand our viewpoint to include seeing smoking not as a problem, but as an activity engaged in by an entirely loveable human being living life as best he can, we have denied smoking problem status.

We did nothing about the "problem". We didn't fix it, in fact we realise that it doesn't need to be fixed, nor can it be fixed.

What we did is move beyond our rigid beliefs that we were unlovable and bad. Those same beliefs were disguised as trying to do something to benefit us, such as berating us for smoking.

We come to understand that we don't have a problem to fix. That's the problem fixed.

We stop criticising us and others follow.

Happiness shows up when we stop insisting upon it.

We become enlightened when we accept un-enlightenment, for accepting un-enlightenment may be the only enlightenment there is.

Chapter 17

Loving smoking

Anything we're doing in our life can be used to learn about who we are and what our life's about. There appears to be no answers, much as we struggle to find them and then defend them. We resort to serious self-delusion in order to maintain our "truths" and "answers".

Answers are expedient decisions made by us for safety. There's no truth in any of them, though their promise of safety may appear temporarily delivered. There's not even a good way of going about the inquiry into our happiness and life purpose. Whatever we bring to the collective exercise is what we should bring. Becoming a Buddhist monk, a jogger, a preacher, a tennis player, a businesswoman, a teacher of God, a housewife, an electrician, a gardener or an actress who smokes, continues our enquiry into the love of self, the love of others and the love of life itself. All of our contributions to the experience of living on Planet Earth are equally valuable, and taken together constitute the human contribution to the Universe.

By being present to, taking responsibility for, and living out our particular journey, we play our small part in the life of the Universe which spawned us. Our particular role is decreed by evolution. It's not ours to determine. By providing a constantly changing environment the Universe provides a territory in which to explore who we are. So much of this is beyond our understanding that it may be best not to try and come to a conclusion about it, but stay available for the next change.

By accepting, nurturing and eventually loving our particular pathway, despite the traumas along the way, we come to love ourselves, others and the world. Those activities which were keeping us away from love fall naturally by the wayside without us having to do anything about them. We bid them adieu with thanks.

What is the role of smoking in the scheme of things?

Tobacco is an organic product which human beings didn't invent and has been used by people for centuries, also part of evolution. We don't know where smoking is headed.

Smoking is an act of love. All acts are acts of love, though in the first instance they may be intended to avoid or deny love. The pain and suffering some acts create highlights our lack of love and may initiate a journey to recover it. I presume that if we humans could love unconditionally, and if that were of value in the scheme of things, then that would be the case.

Exploring love, without intention, allows love to reveal itself.

Next time you feel the urge to smoke, notice yourself or others smoking, or feel the need to judge smoking in ourselves or others, become aware of love's presence.

Allow your concern with smoking to anchor love's presence.

The arrival of love heralds the departure of fear, judgement, the need to look good and the need for separateness from our fellow beings.

We can use smoking to breathe in a life so charged with love that we lose our attachment to living. By losing the need to live, life blossoms. Within our willingness to own and live out our own part of the journey, love blooms.

We watch ourselves, with increasing peace and growing reverence, being in love.

Epilogue

Work was such fun and we'd known each other for so long that the changes taking place in his behaviour went largely unnoticed. It was only in the aftermath of the Rochester affair that we'd become aware of the difference in the way he was acting. Now it seemed obvious. Rochester was one takeover where we'd expected him to come out with guns blazing, as he'd done so often and so successfully in the past. Our group had created its market niche by just such aggressive and timely manoeuvres. We'd never questioned his strategy or his assessment of the players, nor had the market, and what other judge was there?

Now he seemed less intent on winning, somehow more remote. Not that I noticed hesitancy in his step, or his dealings. There was none. If anything he'd lost the brooding we'd come to recognise heralded a run on the market in one direction or another as he geared up again to test himself against the best. Now he was less obsessed with outcomes, less opinionated, and often seemed content not to know, where knowing and acting early had paid such handsome dividends over the years. His management of the team was legendary in a field in which mavericks ruled. We'd come to trust his steely nerve implicitly. Now it was replaced with a flexibility, even a softness which intrigued, and at the same time bothered, every one of us. Where he'd previously been determined to achieve results he now seemed unconcerned. He traded as if there was no preferred outcome.

We watched intently for signs of internal conflict, asking him if there was anything wrong. We could see that he wasn't entirely settled, but there was more a sense of inquiry about him than anxiety. Frankly it fascinated us, even more than it perturbed us.

We watched him over the next few months, each of us intrigued in our own way, each with our own questions and often with our own temporary answers. It was hard to stop trying to work him out, though more often than not today's conclusions were superseded by tomorrow's responses.

Was he having a breakdown? Was he becoming senile?

At fifty?

Did he know what he was doing?

There were times when he was positively glowing, and at times uneasy, yet not once did we see any intention to return, to go back to being the maestro of the markets he once conducted. If he was inclined to use his past experience in times of crisis, we saw no evidence of it. Everything seemed to be changing. Even his famous sense of the outrageous was more infectious than ever. We laughed like never before and loved it.

He was working with an unusual acceptance, as though someone or something was directing him and he was excited and even fulfilled by simply following. For the first time in all those years he appeared to have relinquished the all-consuming need for control. He was increasingly unobtrusive in the office and it seemed, in his own life. Often we'd only realise he was at work by the lingering smell of the cigarettes he'd sworn so many times to give up.

Eventually he stopped pouring over the analysis of the day's trading, accepting without reproach certain of our naïve manoeuvres which in earlier years would have brought a stinging rebuke to the manager and the staff all the way down to the messenger boy. Interestingly, none of us slackened off, much as we'd tried to get away with murder in the past.

We were becoming part of a way of being within which he, and somehow us, felt an unexpected sense of satisfaction. We were both in awe of this process and somewhat concerned at the outcome of it. It wasn't an unpleasant state of anticipation and we eased what fears we had by talking about it amongst ourselves whenever we could. It became the topic of conversation at all of our gatherings. Our partners and friends became as engrossed in proceedings, or at our retelling of them, as we were ourselves. We were surprised at the excitement that we all felt.

The usual indicators of his presence became fewer, though we intuitively seemed to know when he was about.

At year's end, typically our busiest period, even the tell tale cigarette smoke had gone. Nothing was said, unlike the heralding of the semi successful attempts to give up in previous years. It was as though he hadn't given up.

He'd been given up, if you like, without effort. I'm not sure if he was even aware he'd stopped, or if he had.

The office was almost running itself when he told us he was leaving. There was no anger, boredom, nor, when we queried him, a better offer or new interest. There appeared to be no good reason to move on and none was given. In truth, nobody needed to ask. The whole affair felt predestined, begun all those months ago with a certain inevitability, even then.

Events seemed guided by the unknown and consistent with some greater order. All seemed to be in place. At work, life went on, never without a great sense of fun and sometimes with the panic of old, yet with a deep sense of beginning. No one pretended to know what was really happening. We talked about it for several months after he left but that too stopped, for the words no longer represented what we meant.

We'd stopped being concerned with what didn't matter, and in the clearing that was left a new sense of ourselves and our lives appeared. Previous anxieties gave way to an increasing sense of well-being and a sense of deep belonging, and I know I speak for all of us when I say an ever increasing compassion and gratitude. Our early sadness at his departure lifted to reveal a joy few of us had known, for somehow his absence welcomed into our lives, and nurtured within us, the presence of the divine.

The End

Made in the USA
San Bernardino, CA
13 June 2017